Praise for
The Healing Choice

"A rare, close-up view of the healing journey. Brenda's and Susan's parallel journeys—of wrestling with God and of finding support in the community of women—speak of hope in the midst of brokenness, acceptance in the face of unbelievable pain. Rather than allowing the devastation to crush their lives, these bold women chose to place their broken hearts and unmet dreams in God's holy hands. With amazing vulnerability, they show how wives can restore their fractured hearts, recover shattered marriages, and find help and healing regardless of their husband's choices."

—BARBARA ROSBERG, cohost of the nationally syndicated radio show *Dr. Gary and Barb, Your Marriage Coaches* and coauthor of *Six Secrets to a Lasting Love*

"What an empowering, freeing book! In *The Healing Choice,* Brenda and Susan open their lives and share how our choice to be whole is not dependent on the actions or choices of our husbands. Healing can begin now! Your life is not on hold until your husband is free. Freedom is yours regardless of where your husband is on his journey. Brenda and Susan, thanks for reaching beyond your pain to pour life into others."

—LISA BEVERE, speaker, cofounder of Messenger International, and author of *Fight Like a Girl* and *Kissed the Girls and Made Them Cry*

"This book hits very close to home. Fred's and Clay's struggle with lust and pornography are very similar to mine. And just like Susan, my wife came to the realization that to heal from such a deception can only come from a deeper walk and intimacy with our Lord and Savior Jesus Christ. Brenda reminds all of us that nothing can separate us from the love of Christ, and no matter what horrible circumstances we may end up facing, whether a drawn-out, tragic death of a dear loved one or a husband who has broken his marriage vows time and time again, Christ ultimately provides our hope of survival. Thank you, Brenda and Susan, for sharing your hearts with us so we can see how the power of God truly transforms people here on earth."

—MICHAEL O'BRIEN, singer, songwriter, and musician,
and former lead singer of Newsong

"Although it can certainly feel like an overwhelming challenge, complete forgiveness and healing *isn't* an unattainable goal. Let Brenda and Susan's insightful book walk you through the restoration process step by step. It's a journey you'll be forever glad you made."

—SHANNON ETHRIDGE, MA, best-selling author of the
Every Woman's Battle series and *Completely His: Loving Jesus Without Limits*

"The Stoekers and Allens continue to provide a message of wholeness to all who have been fortunate enough to experience their writings. Their contributions to the body of Christ have been and continue to be immeasurable."

—MARK GUNGOR, author of *Laugh Your Way to a Better Marriage*

"If a spouse has tragically betrayed you, then *The Healing Choice* is one of the most important books you will ever pick up. The authors, Brenda and Susan, will sensitively come alongside you in one of the darkest times of your life and then guide you through what can be a powerfully redeeming journey. Their wisdom comes not only out of their own pain but also from the grace that helped them and those they've supported to embrace restoration and hope."

—RANDY PHILLIPS, DD, former president of Promise Keepers
and president of Passage

The Healing Choice

Find INTIMACY, CONNECTION,
and FREEDOM regardless
of his choices

The
Healing Choice

How to Move
Beyond Betrayal

BRENDA STOEKER
and SUSAN ALLEN

WATERBROOK
PRESS

THE HEALING CHOICE
PUBLISHED BY WATERBROOK PRESS
12265 Oracle Boulevard, Suite 200
Colorado Springs, Colorado 80921
A division of Random House Inc.

This book is not intended to replace the medical advice of a trained medical professional. Readers are advised to consult a physician or other qualified health-care professional regarding treatment of their medical problems. The author and publisher specifically disclaim liability, loss, or risk, personal or otherwise, which is incurred as a consequence, directly or indirectly, of the use or application of any of the contents of this book.

All Scripture quotations, unless otherwise indicated, are taken from the Holy Bible, New International Version®. NIV®. Copyright © 1973, 1978, 1984 by International Bible Society. Used by permission of Zondervan Publishing House. All rights reserved. Scripture quotations marked (AMP) are taken from The Amplified® Bible. Copyright © 1954, 1958, 1962, 1964, 1965, 1987 by The Lockman Foundation. Used by permission. (www.Lockman.org). Scripture quotations marked (NASB) are taken from the New American Standard Bible®. © Copyright The Lockman Foundation 1960, 1962, 1963, 1968, 1971, 1972, 1973, 1975, 1977, 1995. Used by permission. (www.Lockman.org). Scripture quotations marked (NKJV) are taken from the New King James Version®. Copyright © 1982 by Thomas Nelson Inc. Used by permission. All rights reserved. Scripture quotations marked (TLB) are taken from The Living Bible, copyright © 1971. Used by permission of Tyndale House Publishers Inc., Wheaton, Illinois 60189. All rights reserved.

Italics in Scripture quotations reflect the authors' added emphasis.

Details in some anecdotes and stories have been changed to protect the identities of the persons involved.

ISBN 978-1-4000-7425-9

Published in the United States by WaterBrook Multnomah, an imprint of The Doubleday Publishing Group, a division of Random House Inc., New York.

WATERBROOK and its deer design logo are registered trademarks of WaterBrook Press.

Library of Congress Cataloging-in-Publication Data
Stoeker, Brenda.
    The healing choice : how to move beyond betrayal / by Brenda Stoeker and Susan Allen. — 1st ed.
        p. cm.
    ISBN 978-1-4000-7425-9
  1. Wives—Religious life. 2. Christian women—Religious life. 3. Husbands—Sexual behavior.
4. Sex—Religious aspects—Christianity. 5. Betrayal. I. Allen, Susan, 1954– II. Title.

    BV4528.15.S76 2008
    248.8'435—dc22

                                        2007051401

Printed in the United States of America
2008—First Edition

10 9 8 7 6 5 4 3 2 1

Contents

Introduction

by Fred Stoeker

Not long ago, lung cancer stalked my mother-in-law, Gwen Hulett, and finally crushed the life out of her. Satan spent that same withering year sifting my wife, Brenda, like harvest wheat while Gwen was torn slowly, agonizingly from her hands. I've never observed a closer mother-daughter relationship. Brenda's mother was her dearest friend.

I haven't forgotten how harrowing it was to look into Brenda's eyes back then. Horrific things lurked behind the windows to her soul—things I never dreamt I'd see, like the raw anger that flashed one night when I gathered the kids around to worship and to pray for Gwen's healing. Brenda spat, "I'm not going to worship a God who would allow this to happen to me!" Gritting her teeth, she crossed her arms, her steely eyes ablaze.

At other times, I saw in those eyes the lost, vacant confusion of a bag lady unable to cope with the complexities of life. Brenda simply couldn't face her mother's suffering. Agonizing regret and constant guilt over her responses to Gwen's diagnosis pillaged her peace of mind. Brenda's trust in God was weighed on the scales and found wanting, and her emotional collapse left her unable to care for her mother as she wanted to. The resulting shame and self-condemnation tormented my wife night and day.

But most harrowing to me was when I searched those lovely green eyes for my Brenda and found no one home. Her smile was lifeless; her mood unresponsive. The Brenda I'd known was now gone, somewhere far, far away. I knew we'd pass through this yawning bleakness together, but would I recognize my wife on the other side?

I'm very grateful that, though it took a little time, my Brenda is back, and her smile is just as mesmerizing as ever. To me—and to her—everything seems new again, even her perspective. This was illustrated to me not long ago when we strolled hand in hand through our neighborhood on an orange-tinged autumn afternoon.

"You know what?" she said, suddenly breaking the silence. "This grief process has parallels to the emotional mess a wife goes through when she catches her husband in sexual sin. You would be amazed."

I stopped in my tracks. It was an incredible thought in its own right, but it seemed somehow more incredible coming from Brenda. Brenda has always been more into human relationships than philosophical musings, so this tying together of unrelated topics like a mother's death and a husband's sexual sin was not her normal gig. *But something has changed,* I thought as we resumed our walk.

Sure, I suppose everyone tends to think deeper thoughts in the wake of a loved one's death, but this seemed like something more to me. Somewhere in the midst of Gwen's sickness, Brenda shifted from deep collapse into high gear with God. From that moment on, I've never seen Brenda so hungry for God, so hungry for the truth. This conversation, like so many others in past months, showed me that not only was my old Brenda back, but she was also a deeper, more resilient woman, sure of where she stood with God. For me, her husband of nearly twenty-five years, she was now more like a Brenda-on-spiritual-steroids, an even more intriguing wife than the one I knew before. All the confusion, dread, and loneliness she felt when she entered a private world of grief had dissipated like a summertime cloudburst.

"I don't get it," I commented. "I mean, I understand how a wife grieves the loss of her dreams for marriage, but what you said makes it sound as if the parallels go deeper than that."

Brenda thought a moment. "Think about it like this," she began. "What I experienced was the most earth-shattering, life-changing kind of pain. I don't think I could ever experience anything harder than that… Mom's sickness was just hideously awful. What's worse, I was completely unprepared to handle what happened to me. I had no intention of taking that journey, but I wasn't given a choice. One day Mom seemed fine; the next day I found out she was dying, which thrust me into a horrid wilderness without warning and with only the spiritual resources I had on me at the time. Remember how betrayed I felt by the Lord, and how that betrayal twisted me into someone else?"

"Yes, I remember," I said, nodding for her to go on.

"I just didn't have enough of what I needed spiritually to survive, so I had to scratch up what I needed along the way, turning my whole focus upon the Lord. The same thing has to be true for a wife who is enduring the pain of a husband's unfaithfulness. She has to be experiencing the most shattering, deepest kind of pain she might ever encounter, but she has no more choice in it than I had. One day her marriage seems normal, and the next day perversion breaks out everywhere. She is likely unprepared for the crushing pain of betrayal that has her buried deep in an emotional wasteland without a clue how to get out. Perhaps for the first time, she's finding out exactly what her spiritual resources amount to. What happens if she doesn't have what she needs to pull through and get her heart back?"

I shrugged blankly.

"Don't you see?" Brenda asked. "Once that storm crashes in and she realizes she doesn't have the connection with God she needs to handle this kind of trauma, she has to immediately begin building up spiritual resources and her own intimacy with God, just like I did in the middle of my grief. Otherwise, she may be twisted into something she doesn't want to be by the bitterness of it all. Sure, the husband's decisions will determine what happens to him and to the family in the long run, but when it comes to restoring her *own* heart, it won't be what God does in her husband that will determine who she becomes on this journey. It will be what she chooses to allow God to do in her along the way, before her husband even changes! God will want to use that journey to grow her, just like He used the grief over Mom to grow me. But she'll have to choose to move into God with all of her heart. That's the key, and that's where the parallel lies. I learned so much about healing my heart, even in the middle of chaos. I think I could also help any wife dealing with her husband's betrayal."

I was fascinated. As I walked on with Brenda, my thoughts bounced back to an e-mail from Angie that had hit my in box just that morning:

> I am desperate for a pinpoint of hope right now. Though I am just married, my husband's porn and lust are killing our marriage. I have been so completely deceived and lied to that I've become someone else, someone I don't want to be. I have never been so hurt, wounded, frustrated, and hopeless. My husband is a believer and knows all the right words to say about this issue, but the sin continues daily (if not hourly), and he continues to lie to me about it and to deceive himself by saying he "isn't as bad as the next guy." We have been to counseling, but that only worked for a day.
>
> I can no longer handle this issue on my own. I am desperate for someone to show my husband the depth and weight of his sin. I need encouragement and counseling myself. This is a nightmare compared to my Christian dreams of marriage. I had no idea what I was getting myself into when I said, "I do."

The sentence that struck me was this: "I've become someone else, someone I don't want to be." An unintended journey—a wrenching trial, a blistering betrayal—creates a new person of any one of us and

Introduction   5

can tie a relationship with God into knots. Brenda certainly became someone she didn't want to be, but by God's grace, she found the way back home.

I felt sure there were lessons in her journey that could help lead young wives like Angie back to normal too. But now Brenda had me thinking I could hope for something more. Perhaps someone like Angie could find her healing *before* her twisting ride was over, like Brenda did. Maybe she didn't have to wait for her husband to change after all.

I recalled Brenda's goal for our first book together, *Every Heart Restored*. She wanted that book to help wives restore their hearts completely right in the middle of that nightmare, regardless of whether their husbands repented of their sin or not. At the time, I thought her goal was quite noble, but not quite possible.

But that was then, I reasoned. *How can I doubt anymore? I've just seen someone do it.* Early on, Brenda's soul ran off to who knows where as she teetered at the point of mental collapse. Yet, against all odds, she reversed course and began growing so strong spiritually that by the time I stood before two hundred people at Gwen's funeral, I could honestly open my eulogy with these words:

> I just want to stop a moment to acknowledge my wife's greatness today. Brenda, at the beginning I wasn't sure you were ever going to make it through all this, but I stand here today a very fortunate man. Of all the people who presently live on the earth, only I have been allowed to see what you've gone through this past year. Only I've seen the desperate, endless, persistent work you've put into rebuilding your faith in the wake of that cancer diagnosis. I just want you to know, sweetheart, that it's an honor to walk at your side. And now that we're at the end of this, all I can say is that you've been matchless. What a woman you are, and what a Christian!

Brenda had managed to heal her heart, even though her mom was never healed of that awful cancer. Can a wife also heal her heart, even if her husband never turns from his sexual sin?

As Brenda and I finished our walk that day in the Iowa sunshine, I could only answer yes, completely convinced that Brenda's road map would be an invaluable help to any wife finding herself in that position of betrayal.

The timing of Brenda's insight couldn't have been more perfect either, as God's daughters were lying heavily upon my heart again, just as they were before we wrote *Every Heart Restored*. I knew that meant we'd be writing another book to them very soon, and it was no secret what the Lord had in mind for this one.

In *Every Heart Restored* we stressed two keys to restoring a heart: The first was the need to get more intimate with God than ever before. The second was to build or get involved with a support group.

We hadn't been able to provide the details of how a woman might find this greater intimacy with God in the first book, nor did we offer any details about building support groups, mostly because Brenda and I believed the groups would spring up naturally. That's what happened with the men's groups after my book *Every Man's Battle*. Why not with the ladies? But for whatever reason, hurting women did not find or form support groups as easily as the men did. Still, their e-mails convinced us that many hurting wives would be willing to risk starting a group if they just had a little guidance up front.

The big question for me was: *How can we help women deal with this pair of deeper healing issues?* Once Brenda shared her insight into the parallels between grief and sexual sin, I realized I had my answer on the first issue. I was certain Brenda could teach any woman how to build up intimacy with God, no matter what kind of nightmare she was enduring.

But what of building support groups? Neither Brenda nor I had any experience with support groups. Well, thank God for Clay and

Susan Allen. When it comes to the passion for sexual purity, Clay and I are identical twins, peas in a pod, cut from the same cloth—you name the cliché—except for one crucial difference. I had walked into sexual freedom on my own, alone in Christ, a story I shared in *Every Man's Battle*. Clay's was a team story, as he found his freedom through Christian community—a life-giving connection that's part of healthy support groups. After learning of Clay's addiction to porn, Susan restored her heart in that same kind of community through the help of other hurting sisters in Christ.

Before long, Clay and Susan began leading their own groups. Then they created a nonprofit organization called Avenue to distribute support-group curricula and provide mentoring help to group leaders through their volunteer staff in California.

Within the first ten minutes of our phone call to Clay and Susan, Clay told me he had been praying for some time that God would provide him with an ally for his ministry, because he felt that if those of us teaching about sexual purity would team up instead of working separately, we could really put the Enemy on the run. That was all I needed to hear. An alliance was born.

The book you're holding is the first fruit of this young relationship. It lays out the practical steps you can take to restore your heart—both as an individual and as a member of a support community. In part 1 of the book, Brenda shares her story of losing her mother to cancer. What she learned applies to anyone facing unbearable pain and especially the "cancer" of sexual sin. She shares how she resolved feelings of betrayal and intense anger with God in the midst of her unintended journey. Then in part 2, Susan Allen talks about her own experiences and about building support to get you moving in the right direction fast.

It is our sincere hope that their stories will deliver all of the encouragement and advice you need to choose healing and growth through your own unintended journey.

Part 1

❁

Brenda's Story

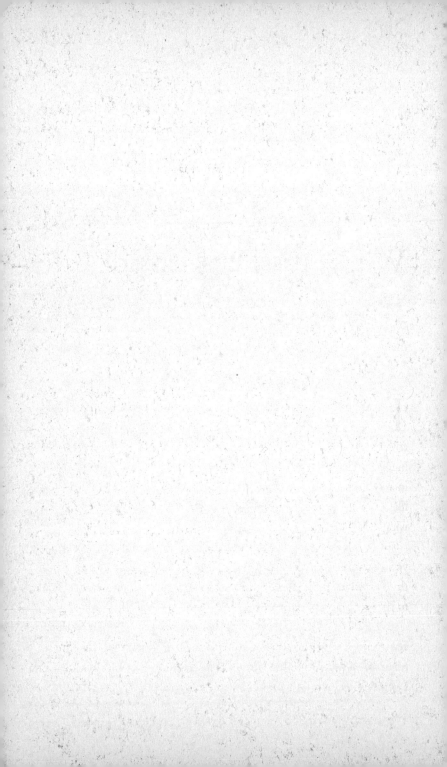

When It's Dark Inside

We strongly recommend that you read
the introduction before reading chapter 1.

It was a blistering, boiling Memorial Day on Louisiana's western border, and for the seventy-five or so members of the Bronson family congregated at Toledo Bend Reservoir for their reunion, time was moving along briskly. The gathering was alive with long-lost cousins laughing, knee-slapping uncles swapping fishing tales, and older aunts giggling like schoolgirls, trading stories and snapshots of grandbabies far and wide. Mom's family reunion was in full swing.

This was a side of Mom's family I'd never known, and many years—at least thirty—had passed since she had gotten together with this branch of her extended family. I had no idea how close she had been to these relatives as a girl.

Mom wasn't the sort to ask favors of us kids—after all, we were adults with our own families—but after getting word of this family reunion, she asked my brother Brent and me if we would fly down to Louisiana with her so she wouldn't have to go alone. We knew that this weekend meant a lot to her, so we quickly agreed to accompany her to the reunion.

I was especially glad we did, because I saw a brand-new side of Mom there. She had always been a bit on the reserved side, but sometime that afternoon, she flicked her "Georgia Peach" charm—Mom was a native of Brunswick, Georgia—to full power. Bubbly, perky, smiling, and laughing, she was the life of the party.

I silently marveled, *You know, she must have been as close to her cousins growing up as I was to mine!* I couldn't recall Mom being that happy and cheerful, so social and outgoing, in all of my life.

In fact, she was so outgoing that when the sun set and the moon rose over the lake, I thought we might have to camp out in the park! She was having so much fun, we could barely get her into the car and out of the park before the gates were locked for the night. During the hourlong trip back to the hotel, she bubbled on about the day. I always loved seeing Mom have a good time, especially since she'd been a widow for more than twenty-five years.

A SUMMERTIME COLD

A few weeks after that reunion weekend, Mom caught a bad cold. She eventually recovered, but I was troubled. People rarely get colds in the middle of June when the weather is slowly heating up to blast-furnace levels in the Midwest. A week later, Mom told me she couldn't breathe very well, which raised another alarm since she had never been one to idly complain about her health.

I made a trip to Moline to check up on her—and I was surprised by what I witnessed. Mom, sixty-seven years old, was an active senior who faithfully exercised at the YMCA, but I noticed that she could hardly climb the stairs to the elevated track without having to stop to catch her breath along the way. The next day she was washing windows and had to stop often to rest as she worked her way around the house. That wasn't like Mom at all, as *rest* had always been a four-letter word to her when there was work to be done. Her lack of stamina concerned me.

I figured that a touch of pneumonia had settled into her chest near the end of her cold. I strongly urged her to see the doctor. Mom never liked doctor visits, but after I nagged her to make an appointment, she relented and saw her family doctor. An x-ray report revealed fluid in her lungs. Since the Fourth of July weekend was just around the corner, her doctor set an appointment the following week to have the fluid drained from her lungs and told her to stay home for the weekend and rest. I informed Mom that I'd be back after the Fourth to go with her to her appointment.

My family stayed in Des Moines over the Fourth of July weekend, and I remember thinking as I looked at Fred and the kids goofing around the house, *I really need to enjoy this time.* I don't know if it was intuition or a whisper from the Lord, but I just had a sense that this might be the last fun holiday we'd have for a while and I needed to pay attention to every detail and enjoy myself while everything was still the same.

I drove to Moline the following week to take Mom to the local hospital, where she was to have the fluid drained. Sure enough, her doctor extracted a full seventeen hundred cc's. The procedure was very painful, as evidenced by her slow, measured steps between the hospital and the car. After I drove Mom home, I gave her the maximum dose of pain medication and tucked her into bed. It would take some time for her lungs to recover from the procedure, but I knew she would be okay after a few days of rest. Since I didn't need to be underfoot, I kissed her goodbye and headed home to Des Moines.

A few days later, Mom called and told me that her doctor had the test results on the fluid from her lungs and had asked Mom to come into the office to discuss them. Mom paused. Then she asked me, "Can you come over to Moline for the appointment? The doctor said it would be best for me to bring a family member."

Terror struck my heart. I knew exactly what it means when you're told to bring along a family member—a life-threatening disease, probably cancer. Up until that point, I hadn't given that possibility much thought. Sure, her doctor had included cancer as one of the possible causes of the fluid, but that seemed like such a remote possibility because of Mom's vitality. She had seemed so full of life in Louisiana, and everything was fine until that cold hit her in June.

Fred and I jumped into the car, and Brent and his daughter Christina also came down from Chicago to attend Mom's appointment with the doctor. I'm afraid I didn't handle the situation very well. I could barely sit still in the crowded waiting room, and when they called us back to the examination room, I could hardly rise to my feet. As Fred half-carried me down the hall, I felt like I was marching blindfolded before a firing squad, where I would await the crack of a rifle round to end life as I knew it.

The wait for the doctor to come into the room was paralyzing. Unable to face my fears, I leaned my head on Fred's shoulder. I was unresponsive, practically catatonic from fear that the prognosis—verdict— would be a death sentence.

Mom's doctor entered the cold, sterile examination room and quickly got down to business. She reached for a folder, scanned a few lines, and then looked at Mom. "Mrs. Hulett, I regret to inform you that the biopsy results report that you have cancer. The test results didn't reveal what type of lung cancer it is, so as yet I have no prognosis for you. I'll recommend an oncologist for you today, and he will order some further tests that will help determine your next course of action."

Mom's doctor exuded all the warmth of a bank officer announcing the terms of a house refinance loan. I don't remember what transpired over the next few minutes. All I recall is Brent mumbling something to the doctor as Fred pulled me gently to my feet. I somehow stood without keeling over and finally found Mom's hand as we walked out in a state of shock and got into our van. I glanced over at Mom and saw that her fingers twitched and fidgeted nervously. I had never seen her have a nervous mannerism, so I knew that her mind had to be running at a zillion miles per hour after hearing that diagnosis. Perhaps she was recalling her dad's death to cancer, which was so torturous that near the end the nurse complained that he'd become so thin she could hardly find a place to stick the needle for the pain shots.

She had watched cancer devour her cherished husband, Frank—my dad—as well. She had also witnessed the transformation of her strapping brother Don to a skeletal shell. Another brother, Charles, faced the ravages of this deadly disease as well. When he was on his deathbed at home, Mom asked a visiting nurse why her smiley brother always had a frown on his face as he slept. The nurse instantly increased his pain medication, saying simply, "The frowns mean pain." Charles died a few days later, hemorrhaging and gagging on his own blood.

Yes, Mom understood cancer's death sentence well, but I'm sure that as her fingers twitched on the ride home that morning, she couldn't fathom the agony she was about to endure.

A Treatment Plan

After absorbing the initial shock, the family regrouped to discuss our options. We decided to get Mom into the oncologist as soon as possible to learn exactly what we were up against.

The lung specialist who examined Mom performed a biopsy to determine the type of cancer she had. We hoped the results from the biopsy would help us build a treatment strategy. While we waited for those results, the doctor said he had to attempt to seal the lining of her lungs to prevent fluids from building up again. The procedure involved the painful insertion of a chest tube for drainage. My younger brother, Barry, came up from Kansas City and offered to spend the week with her in Moline while she recovered. Brent came down for the day too, but I just couldn't face it, so I stayed in Des Moines. The oncologist showed my brothers an x-ray of her lungs and pointed out the cancer's whitish sandpaper appearance. Both lungs seemed full of cancer. To this day, I'm glad I never saw that x-ray.

But that was just a taste of the horrors that awaited us. To my sensibilities, setting a chest tube was about as artful as jamming a tube into a Vermont maple tree to draw off syrup. The doctor admitted as much, telling my brothers that he never knew exactly what the experience would be like for the patient. As fate would have it, the chest tube insertion was a horrible event for us. Essentially by chance, the doctor jammed the chest tube tightly against a nerve, which was so excruciatingly painful for Mom that she could barely eat over the next week.

Still, I had no idea of the scope of what Mom was enduring until I arrived at the end of the week to relieve my brother and found her lying in bed, moaning and groaning. Knowing that ordinarily she was a very tough person who could endure intense pain without letting on, I realized the situation was extremely rough for her.

I spent the afternoon calling various doctors to get the pain medication increased, but they wouldn't give her anything stronger unless she was in the hospital where she could be monitored. Shocked by her condition and fearing that something was dreadfully wrong, I called Brent to discuss the situation. We both agreed that I should drive her to the emergency room; her pain was that serious. Nearing the midnight hour, I gingerly helped Mom into the van and escorted her to the hospital.

We were both hoping that the ER docs would agree that, yes, she should be hospitalized so that trained medical personnel could monitor her pain until it was time to remove the chest tube. They didn't choose that course of action, however. Instead, they gave her a shot of morphine and sent us home, despite our pleas for her to be admitted.

Feeling defeated, I stayed with Mom, but it was extremely traumatic for me. I was frightened to see how fast she'd declined. She was a small person to begin with, but she had lost a lot of weight. On top of that, the massive doses of pain medication were causing delusions and hallucinations. A lot of what Mom said didn't make sense, which bothered me so much that I barely slept at night.

Four interminable days later, it was finally time to remove the chest tube and receive the oncologist's report. I told Brent and Barry that I couldn't handle the agony of watching the tube being wrenched from her chest. As for the report, I just couldn't face hearing the bad news that I was expecting. "Could you please go without me?" I asked my brothers. Courageously, they did.

When Brent and Barry returned with Mom after the first appointment, they rushed her to her bedroom so she could lie down. She looked pale, weak, and withdrawn. My brothers told me that the removal of the tube had been unbearably painful for Mom. The doctors ripped the tube out quickly, just like a nurse tearing a Band-Aid off a scab, and Mom yelped out in pain.

An hour later, my brothers had to get Mom out of bed for the appointment with the oncologist. With my heart in my throat, I watched them drive away and wondered how life would be changed upon their return. I feared the worst, the absolute worst.

With some time on my hands, I walked out back to sit underneath the patio overhang. I just sat there frozen, thinking over the past parade of time. The house at 815 54th Street B was not just Mom's house. It was the house Dad built with his own hands, the house we'd grown up in. I loved our home and the forested ravine behind our well-kept garden and backyard. *This will probably be the last time I sit here like this in this place,* I thought. *My whole life is going away. If Mom dies, we'll have to sell this house, the place that has been my home forever. All the happy years and memories that are wrapped up in it will be gone.* For that one afternoon, before I knew the full answer on her cancer, I needed to sit there and soak in the memories stirred by all that surrounded me. Sitting on that patio was one of those heavy, bittersweet moments in life.

I walked to a hanging basket, which contained the most gorgeous rose bloom, and I just gazed and admired it. I then regarded the other flowers in their planters and pondered all the years I'd spent in that backyard. I walked over to the ravine and reflected upon the beauty and tranquillity of the open space behind our backyard. I saw the crab apple tree that Fred had planted with such effort on the steepest part of the hillside, as well as the evergreen he had lovingly placed in the ground at Mom's request. I saw the markers for our Boston terriers, which we had buried there years ago when I was a teenager. That afternoon I was reminded of how blessed we had been as a family, so I was also painfully aware of everything I stood to lose.

Fear of the utter loss and devastation we were facing began to take over my life completely, causing me to wonder if I could even get through this experience without going out of my mind. I had already lost Dad way too many years ago. The thought of losing Mom terrorized my soul. You see, all my life I had experienced unconditional love from both my parents. Few can say that, and I knew how blessed I was. It didn't matter that I wasn't a superstar at sports or in music, and it didn't matter whether I was beautiful or popular in high school, either. I was average in everything I did, but that didn't matter to my parents. They loved me deeply, and they let me know often of their love and support for me.

Mom never criticized my parenting, even when Fred or I still had to lie down next to our firstborn son, Jasen, to get him to take his nap as a two-year-old. Mom could have told us we were going about it all wrong, but she didn't. She was just always there whenever we called, ready and available. She never made us feel like she had anything more important to do than talk to us. When our younger son, Michael, was so difficult during the terrible twos, Mom offered to live with us so she could lend a hand around the house. She was generous too. One time, when I wrecked the van and ruined our only way to get to Florida for vacation, she bought six airline tickets so we wouldn't miss our annual trip to the beach.

The more I recalled these precious memories, the more paralyzing the tension became within me as I awaited the return of Mom and my brothers. I decided to clean house, because my aunt Barbara always told me that whenever she had a lot on her mind, she would vacuum, mop, and straighten up the house to take her mind off her troubles.

THE VERDICT

While dusting in the living room, I heard the front door open. I rushed to greet them, only to witness my brothers bringing Mom in and heading directly to her room so she could lie down. When I sat down next to her, she just looked up and said, "Well, it wasn't good. We just have to make the most of what time we have left." She had started out with a brave smile, but it crumpled quickly as tears began pouring down her cheeks.

Barry explained that she had mesothelioma, the worst kind of lung cancer. It was already at stage three or four on a scale of four, and there was no available treatment for it. The doctor gave us six months or less.

I collapsed on Mom, crying as if my heart would burst. My brothers sat down next to me and put their arms around me, and the four of us just cried and cried. When our tears were spent, we discussed what to do next. She was so sick that I didn't think I could stay and handle her care all by myself in Moline. I figured that if I took her to Des Moines, I would have Fred's help and could continue to maintain a semblance of normal life, like getting the kids ready for school and helping them with their homework after dinner. Just being in my own house would make it easier for me to cook and care for her. I'd be better able to build up her weight and help her recover from the chest-tube removal that had been so hard on her.

The decision made, we gathered a few things, and after settling her in the car for the trip to Des Moines, I walked out back to take one more look at the beautiful rose in the hanging basket that I'd admired earlier in the day. In just those few hours, the whole bloom had withered and fallen off. That unusual sight struck me as a terrible omen of what we were about to go through.

By the time we got home, Mom was so weak that Fred and I had to practically carry her downstairs to the basement guest room. It took me less than twenty-four hours to realize that caring for her in Des Moines would be much harder than I had anticipated. Mom was totally dependent, and there was the bite of reality I'd failed to anticipate: the kids had never experienced a close family member's dealing with a terminal illness, so they were suffering with deep needs too. Besides that, Mom was so debilitated that first week that I was convinced she would die at any moment. As a registered nurse, I knew that most people with this kind of aggressive cancer usually didn't survive six months. Most only lived a month or two after a diagnosis of a terminal disease. I was horrified, petrified. *She's going to die right in front of me, right in my own house!*

Because Mom's situation seemed to be going downhill quickly, we immediately called Mercy Hospice, located just three blocks from us. We had no problem getting in to see the director to discuss what we might expect from mesothelioma, and the hospice people quickly and lovingly sprang into action.

Hospice nurses and social workers began coming regularly, but their presence brought a new wave of trauma into my life. All they talked about was "understanding this process of transition" and "embracing the stages of death." Everything was so matter-of-fact that sometimes I felt like we were discussing nothing more distressing than what we were planning for dinner that night.

But for me, everything was emotionally overwhelming. I had barely begun to process the idea that Mom was going to die, and already, everywhere I turned, I kept getting hit with talk about death. On top of that, my own house had turned against me; every room reminded me that I was living in a death place. Sitting on my night table were hospice booklets about symbolic boats sailing over the horizon into the next life. If I headed downstairs, I'd see stacks of paperwork created by record transfers and medical payments. I'd turn to the family room and see Mom's little table next to the couch piled high with bottles of pills. I'd open the refrigerator and see pinkish bottles of Boost nutritional supplement meant to help Mom get stronger and gain weight. Turning into the dining room, I'd see oxygen tanks stashed in the corner. If I jumped into the car for a quick escape, Mom's handicapped parking permit hanging from the rearview mirror mocked me on my way out the driveway.

Our lives turned upside down, from normal to a horrifying, endless nightmare in which I was forced to watch a beloved friend tortured to death right before my eyes. I went downhill quickly. The stress and the shock were more than I could bear. My odd response was to put some physical—and emotional—distance between me and Mom, my best and dearest friend in the world. I didn't want her to suffer, and most of all, I didn't want to *see* her suffer. I screamed inside, *Lord, after all I've been through with Dad, I don't want to go through this again! Don't let her linger here for a month or two. Just take her now, and get us away from this!*

But then the unexpected happened. Mom didn't die immediately; instead she began to strengthen and gain weight. I should have been happy, but her improved condition only prompted me to avoid her even more. I would stay in different rooms. I would find excuses to leave the house. I couldn't stand it, I couldn't get away from it, and I couldn't come to grips with it. I could not find God. Scriptures and His promises had no effect on me whatsoever. I had no strength spiritually. In fact, I was so enraged at God I could barely contain it.

Those were the blackest of days. I was just being burned alive by the stress. Anxiety would press in on me while I slept and weighed heavily on my shoulders when I was awake. The awfulness was indescribable. I was quickly tossed into a whirlpool of weight loss, dropping twenty-seven pounds in three weeks and eventually falling to four pounds below my wedding weight.

That's when Fred stepped in. He simply said, "I'm taking over. I know Gwen is your mom and not mine, so perhaps I don't have a right to do this, but I'm taking over anyway. I've been waiting for you to get your feet back under you, but it isn't happening."

I was frozen in fear.

"Look in the mirror, sweetheart. You look anorexic, like Karen Carpenter did before she died. That scares me, and it's scaring our friends. I'm taking over, and I will make the decisions that will be best for everyone concerned from here on out. I will also call and tell your brothers about the situation, so you won't have to be embarrassed in any way. They will understand, but if they don't, I'm still taking over. You just rest now. The first decision I'm making is that we are going for counseling immediately. I'm calling Ed and Pat Ashby right now."

FROM FRED

We had sought counseling from the Ashbys in the past and counted them as dear friends. I reached Pat Ashby and briefly explained our situation and my fears regarding Brenda's health.

"I'm booked full today, but have her come in over the lunch hour," she replied. "This sounds pretty serious, and I don't want to wait any longer. After I talk to her, I may need to talk to the both of you together. Will you be available?"

Assuring her that I would be, I gave her my cell number and called Brenda with the news. At noontime, Brenda stepped into Pat's office as I slipped into the prayer room at a nearby church to pray for them. Thirty minutes later, my cell buzzed. "Fred, can you come over to my office right away?" Pat requested. "Brenda and I have made some decisions that will require your help."

I had no idea what to expect as I stepped inside her office, but one look at Brenda's puffy eyes and the mound of crumpled tissues piled at her side told me all I needed to know. My darling wife looked shaken, like a lost and frightened little girl, but I knew she had courageously spilled it all. Pat's grave face also told a story. She was as frightened about Brenda's health as I was.

"Fred, I was horrified when Brenda walked in," she began. Holding her thumb and forefinger a half-inch apart, she continued, "We are this far from having to hospitalize Brenda for her dramatic weight loss, but first I would like to try an alternative route this weekend."

"I'll do anything you recommend, Pat," I assured her.

"Brenda has explained that you've had your mother-in-law living with you for the past six weeks, recovering from that chest-tube surgery, and that you've been trying to get her weight and strength back up again. Like any daughter, Brenda wants to be there for her mother, and Brenda has obviously done a good job caring for her. But while Gwen has been getting stronger and gaining weight, Brenda's health has headed the other direction, spiraling downward. She's been losing weight every single day, and she's admitted to me that she's becoming more and more unstable emotionally."

Pat's certainly got that nailed, I thought as I nodded for her to continue.

"The problem for Brenda is that she's being forced to handle both the grieving role of a daughter and the caregiving role of a nurse. Sometimes that works; sometimes it doesn't. Did you know that studies of terminal patients show that up to one-third of their loved ones cannot emotionally handle the caregiving role?"

Stunned, I shook my head. "I had no idea the number was that high, Pat."

"Well, that's why you and I have got to step in and help Brenda separate this caregiving role from her role as a daughter, at least for the time being. We have to stop this spiral, or else the stress will drive Brenda's health into total collapse."

"So what do we do?" I queried.

"I told you on the phone that we've made some decisions and we need your help. The first step for you will be the easy part. I want you to check Brenda into a hotel for the next three days to separate her from the stress she's feeling at home with her mom's sickness. I suggest the Stoney Creek Inn right up the street. It's the perfect place. She needs to stay there alone and sleep there alone to give her a chance to decompress, and Brenda shouldn't talk to her mom while she's away. While you and the kids can visit, you need to give her plenty of time for sleep and rest."

"We'll do it," I said.

"Great! Now, the second step won't be so easy for you. Your job is to go home and tell a terminally ill patient that she's going to have to move back to Moline and live there alone. Not only that, she'll have to leave your house before Brenda checks out of the hotel Sunday."

Send Gwen home? But she's dying! I could barely grasp what I heard. "How am I supposed to do that?" I asked, a bit shocked. Gwen had saved my bacon early and often in my marriage, and she always treated me like a son. How could I turn my back on her now?

"Fred, I know what you're thinking, but in this situation, you need to be there for your wife," Pat said.

I knew that before you said it, I thought, sighing deeply and gritting my teeth. As much as my heart broke for Gwen, and in spite of my promise that I would fight this cancer every step of the way at her side, my first allegiance was to her daughter—my wife.

On the way home, I checked a teary Brenda into the Stoney Creek Inn with a kiss, promising to return with some clothes and an overnight bag after dropping our bombshell on Gwen. Buckling my seat belt once more, I prayed my way home, crying for answers. *How in the world do I do this?* Once home, I resolutely drew up a chair next to Gwen and outlined the counselor's recommendations. The news shook my mother-in-law to her toes, but as usual, Gwen's greatness made the situation easier.

"We'll have to call Brent and make sure he's here Sunday to pick me up and take me home," she said, gracious to a fault. "I'll make this work, Freddie. My girl's the only thing on my mind right now. We have to get her better."

By Sunday morning, the three days were up, and Brenda had not spoken to her mother since she'd checked into the hotel. My wife knew that Gwen would be worried sick if she didn't hear from her at least once before her departure, so Brenda called my cell just as I was packing Gwen's things into the car. "I made a present for Mom," she informed me. "Could you come over quick and get it from me so she can have it before she goes?"

Since the diagnosis, Gwen had been teaching Brenda to knit. When I got to the hotel, she sniffled tearfully as she handed me a knitted dishrag.

"A dishrag?"

"Don't worry, Fred. Mom will know what I'm trying to say." I knew they were so close that they could communicate without a word, but I also knew that Gwen had a thousand dishrags. How could a dishrag convey anything?

I returned to the house and handed the gift to Gwen. She instantly burst into tears. I managed to give her a hug but then stared blankly. Seeing that I was mystified, she explained, "She's telling me that everything will be okay. Brenda's telling me she's sorry she's let me down, but that she loves me with all of her heart, and she'll see me soon!"

Gwen never stopped clutching that rag; even as she sat in the car, she was dabbing her eyes with it. As the vehicle pulled away, she stuck her head out the window and, with a crooked and painful little smile, called out, "Take care of my girl." The next time I saw that dishrag, it was double-matted and framed, and Gwen told everyone who would listen that it was the most precious gift she'd ever received.

I waved as Brent and Gwen disappeared around the corner, and I somehow held myself together until I stepped through the front door, where I fell to the tile, sobbing with wrenching, inconsolable grief. I felt like I had betrayed my last friend in the world.

I couldn't imagine how Brenda was feeling.

From Brenda

It felt like I was failing everybody. Both Fred and my daughter Rebecca wanted desperately for Mom to stay with us, but because of my inability to handle the stress, I was putting everybody through more pain. Worst of all, Mom was going to have to go home and be on her own.

I'd never felt like such a tremendous failure at any point in my life, and it was crushing. I wanted to withdraw from people. I felt so vulnerable, afraid that even my brothers and cousins would look at me like I was crazy. I should have been stronger. A part of me kept screaming, *I should be able to handle it better! I'm a nurse, for heaven's sake!*

My own words mocked me again and again. For years I told Mom, "It's good that you have a registered nurse as a daughter. If you ever get real sick, I can take care of you!" Now here I was, the vaunted RN who couldn't even stand to hear about her mom's condition, much less be around to care for her.

In her hour of darkest need, I had failed her. She had always been there for me, but when it was my turn to repay her for being my mother all my life, my response was to ship her away from the only place she felt safe. On top of that, I knew my emotional collapse worried her when she had plenty of problems of her own.

I would imagine you're now asking yourself, *What in the world happened to Brenda? Why did she sink so fast?* The answers are instructive to the trauma that you—in all likelihood—are experiencing at this time, as we'll explore in the next chapter.

2

Offended

What in the world happened? How could I—a fourth-generation Christian who never strayed from the straight and narrow all through my school years, including college, who effectively raised four godly children—collapse so quickly, so precipitously?

As horrifically as my grief consumed me, I couldn't blame it all on feelings of sadness, not by a long shot. I'll admit that Mom's terrifying diagnosis of cancer tipped the trajectory of my life into a barrel roll. The anxiety soon had my nose pointing straight at the fast-rising earth, spinning my faith and trust in God into a frightening death spiral.

I fought for some semblance of control by desperately yanking on the controls. I prayed. I repeated Scripture verses over and over, frantically thinking, *Surely God's Word will bring me peace and balance. Yes, I think I can pull out of this spin!*

But it was no use. Against all my expectations, God was not there to hold on to, and His promises to be there when I needed Him most vanished like an early morning mist over an Iowa stream. There simply was no peace. Each time I managed to find some equilibrium, something would send me into another nosedive, tumbling at an even faster rate. Anxiety turned to panic as doom spun ever closer.

Spiritually barren and drained, I finally smashed into the ground at the Stoney Creek Inn, emotionally pulverized. I sensed that at any moment I would lose my mind after only six weeks on this journey of grief. I contemplated a future as an empty shell, bereft of emotions for the rest of my life.

Shaking my head with a wry smirk, I asked myself, *So this is all your Christianity is good for, huh?* Gazing vacantly out my window, I remembered how Fred had tenderly stroked my cheek that morning and looked into my troubled eyes, murmuring, "I can't find you in there anymore, sweetheart!" The eyes are the window of the soul, and all he could see were empty, unfurnished rooms on the other side of the glass.

The grief was crushing, every bit of it. Tears sat behind my eyes every moment of every day. But I was harboring much more than tears.

A bitter, burning fury churned angrily inside me as this thought tormented me continually: *This is not the way Mom's life was supposed to go, and this is not the way a Christian family's life is supposed to look!* Sure, Mom's dad and brothers all succumbed to lung cancer, but Granny lived to be ninety-eight and was quite spry till the end. I expected Mom to live to a ripe old age as her mother had before her, and I had two other good reasons for my expectation.

For one, we as a family needed her, and God had to know that. Because of our public stand for sexual purity in the Every Man's Battle series and our personal commitment to purity in our home, our kids paid a heavy social toll at times, even in church. For instance, our daughter Laura was so iced and isolated by her youth group for her pure stand regarding movies and television that her Christian peers became the most traumatizing force in her life.

As her parents, we knew that frustrating times like this would come, but we also counted on having my mother around to help neutralize these agonizing times in our children's lives with her unconditional love for them. I was certain God understood that, and because His children's needs carry with them an expectation of His provision, we expected Him to provide long life for Mom. Instead, we were handed her grim death sentence.

I also knew that every corner of His Bible promises blessing in return for obedience, and God knew that I'd been careful to love Him and to hold fast to His ways throughout my life (see Deuteronomy 11:22). I was naturally counting on the blessings He'd promised to His obedient children (see verse 27), especially His promise to drive out my enemies that were larger and stronger than I (see verse 23). I had a huge, terrifying enemy—cancer.

Cancer had taken my father, but I knew that God was the loving Father of the fatherless (see Psalm 68:4–6). I absolutely *knew* I couldn't take another devastating bout with cancer, especially one involving my precious mother. I *knew* it would destroy me, and I *knew* He wouldn't ask me to go through that again.

Could I have defended this position if I'd been challenged by a theologian? Probably not, but that didn't matter. In my mind, no loving Father could do such a mean thing to his daughter. In God's kingdom, a daughter's obedience carries with it an expectation of blessing, not disaster.

Still, Mom lay dying of cancer on my couch.

In short, our Christian lives were not playing out the way they were supposed to, at least from my perspective, so I wasn't just crying about this terminal illness. I was furious, utterly offended by God, nearly rabid with rage. *What kind of fraud is this Christianity?*

BEYOND SAD

Three days was a long time to be cooped up in a hotel room, so I did a lot of thinking during my stay at Stoney Creek Inn, reflecting especially upon a riveting question that Pat Ashby had posed over the lunch hour that Friday. "What is it that has taken Gwen's looming death from being simply sad to overwhelming?" she asked.

I instinctively knew what made me feel so sad. The thought of losing Mom brought the sorrow, because the suffering and loss of relationship is always sad. But as normal as my sadness was, there was something quite abnormal in the way I collapsed. I recognized how odd it was, even as it was happening. I just couldn't stop my emotional free fall into that black abyss.

So what took me from merely being sad to overwhelmed? Was it my rage at God? It was critical for me to find an answer, but for the purposes of this book, I'd like to expand Pat's question so that I can help you find the answers you need in your situation. So let's begin with a fundamental question: What takes *any* unintended journey from sad to overwhelming?

To get a handle on this, let's take a peek at two dynamics that occur on these journeys. The first dynamic is pretty easy to spot, and it involves the loss, pain, and change in your horizontal relationships. (Horizontal relationships are with immediate family members and close friends. A vertical relationship is your connection with God.) For example, I experienced trauma upon learning that my mother was terminally ill and from the expectation of the profound sadness that I would feel following the permanent loss of Mom. In the case of your husband's sexual sin, you've encountered the trauma of betrayal and the unsettled future and fading dreams for a now-drifting relationship. This first dynamic brings about the feelings of sadness that all of us experience on these journeys.

The second dynamic revolves around your vertical relationship with God, which involves more theological and psychological questions:

- Does the harsh, new reality of life in the valley match up with what you know about God?
- Is your trust in Him still resolute, or are you confused and disoriented by the gaping inconsistencies you seem to see in Him?

- What kind of God would even allow this rotten journey to start in the first place?

This second dynamic is the one that can blast you right past sadness and into an overwhelming orbit of anger and confusion. When your life takes a seismic hit, the theological disorientation can make it seem like your life no longer looks the way a Christian life is supposed to look. The events happening in your life don't seem to match up with what you've been led to believe about God. You don't know whether it's you who's wrong about God, whether you've been sold a bill of goods, or whether you're just plain going crazy. All you know is that your bedrock faith in God's goodness has become suspect in your eyes. Once that happens, the very foundation of your life will be shaken. That's what happened to me.

When your life is turned upside down, don't be surprised if some of your basic beliefs about God—the ones you learned either as a child or when you became a Christian—are challenged by your trials and tribulations. Perhaps you never imagined that one day cracks would appear in rock-solid, elementary beliefs such as these:

- *God is good at all times. He'll never change.*
- *God is my precious Father, and I'm the apple of His eye. He will complete what He has authored in me, and He'll never love anyone more than He loves me.*
- *Christ overcame the world, but I'll still have trials and tribulations because a third-party intruder (Satan) retains temporary dominion on earth.*

Fundamental truths like these form the theological filters through which we screen events and make sense of our lives. Can these truths be shaken? Not likely when you're sipping a cup of chamomile tea while lounging on your padded chaise in the backyard, a soft leather Bible in your lap and the early Saturday morning sun yawning and stretching through the trees. With your kids sleeping in and your husband racing off to his tee time, you gaze lazily over the gold-plated lip of your teacup while bright goldfinches swoop merrily through the shade to feast at your thistle-seed feeder. Who could feel unsettled about anything at a time like this? Trusting in the Lord is easy when all is right with your world.

But what happens when your life seems to contradict everything the Bible has taught you about God's goodness? How do you feel when you know your family looks nothing like those glossy, smiley family photos printed in brochures and Christian magazines being passed around at church? Your life ought to be working out better, and you probably have a couple of good reasons for believing it should, just like I had.

For one, God knew you needed a high priest and leader for a husband, a spiritual covering over your home and children, the first and last defender of your family's purity. In God's kingdom, His child's needs carry an expectation of His provision. As His child, you naturally expected God's kind provision of a pure high priest. Instead, you got a pornographic-idol worshiper.

God also knew of your commitment to sexual purity. You haven't so much as looked at another man since your wedding day, specifically in obedience to His Word. In God's kingdom, a daughter's obedience carries with it that same expectation of blessing that I'd counted on. As His child, you naturally expected His good blessing—a husband who's as committed to sexual purity as you are. Instead, you've been "graced" with a chronic masturbator.

Notice the parallels with my story? If you are anything like me, your emotions are running parallel with mine as well: *What's up with all this? This stinks!*

If you are offended by God, you might as well admit it, because though you can run, you certainly can't hide on this one. I assure you that if any corner of your house—any part of your relationship with

God—is built upon sand, that corner will wash away with the nasty cascades of emotions flooding through the valley. I know.

Now, that doesn't mean everyone experiences that second dynamic—taking offense with God—on unintended journeys, nor does it necessarily mean you'll react the same way I did. After all, even though Fred and I stood shoulder to shoulder and trudged the same rocky pathways during my mother's journey through the valley of the shadow of death and surveyed the same harsh, frightening landscapes day and night for an entire year, what he saw along the way was completely different from what I saw.

As far as I can tell, not one corner of Fred's house even shifted from the day of Mom's diagnosis until the day she breathed her last. Near the end, when it was apparent that Mom didn't have long to live, we placed her in Mercy Hospice a few blocks from our house. One morning Mom confided to Fred, "You know, Freddie, you come into hospice thinking you're doing it for everyone else, thinking things like, *It's going to be easier for people to take care of me,* or, *It's going to be easier on Brenda, and I'll be close to her home.* And then suddenly you wake up and realize you're in a hospice for only one reason, and that reason is because you're dying." She paused a moment. "And then fear sets in," she whispered.

Fred's heart was wrung into knots by her helpless words, but it didn't reframe his view of God. God was still good. Neither had Fred's trust been shaken on an earlier occasion, when he built a bed in the back of the van and drove Mom eight hours each way to a weekend healing service. Mom was not healed that weekend, but Fred's trust in God was not shaken when his omnipotent God did not overrule Satan and death. He understood God's place, Satan's place, and his own place in the matter.

Sure, Fred was laid low by the sadness like the rest of us. He could barely stand the reality of cancer's finality as he told my mom in tears, "If this cancer winds up taking your life, I can live with that, but I will not be able to put you in the grave in peace unless you give me a chance to fight for your life." I've never seen him fight, fast, and pray with such desperation, his wrenching tears pouring out often with my own.

But Fred never lost sight of the fact that God is trustworthy and loves each one of us dearly. When Mom lay in a coma on her last day of life, my husband sat alone with her early that morning, quietly singing hymns she loved for nearly four hours. He came home glowing because he still knew God was good.

Throughout my mom's final year of life, I witnessed three things about Fred:

- His trust in God's good character never wavered.
- He never doubted God's love for him and for our family, not even for an instant.
- Nothing about the situation raised a single question in his heart.

There was nothing about the way our lives were unfolding that confused Fred, because there was nothing about the harsh reality of Mom's diagnosis that was out of line with Fred's theological filters. God was good, He loved Fred completely, and trials and tribulations had nothing to do with it. Sure, the first dynamic of sadness had its painful way in his horizontal human relationships. But the second dynamic— that theologically disorienting offense with God—never found a footing. It couldn't touch his intimacy with God, and that's how it was supposed to be.

That was not the way everything played out in my life. I had no idea that my own theological filters were so out of kilter with God's truth that a monsoon from the valley of death could leave me unsure that God was even real, much less good. And as for His love for me… well, I wasn't even sure He knew my name.

As far as I was concerned, I was dealing with three issues—betrayal, abandonment, and lack of control.

Betrayal

While Fred was at peace, I was fit to be tied. I saw many things—like betrayal—along our journey that Fred seemed to miss. After living through one cancer death (my dad's), I never wanted to experience cancer up close and personal again. From the day of my father's funeral twenty-four years earlier, that devastating time was a shadowy presence in the back of my mind…always. And whenever that memory slipped to the front of my mind, I would instantly breathe a prayer in my heart: *Lord, please don't let me ever have to go through anything like that again.*

The Lord had to know how desperately I raised that plea, and yet He coldly allowed Mom's cancer to happen anyway. I was outraged and indignant that He would do something that I had specifically prayed against for over twenty-four years, and yet there it sat—cancer on my doorstep, even worse than the time before. At least we'd had some medical treatments to try with Dad. With Mom, there was nothing.

God didn't seem to care a whit about my prayers, and yet praying was all I had left to do. The Lord and I both knew there was no way Mom would live unless He supernaturally healed her, but where would the healing faith come from? He hadn't answered the simple prayer I'd been lifting up for over two decades! What a mockery, and how hopeless!

I was livid. *So I'm the apple of His eye, huh? Whatever!* If He loved me, He never would have heartlessly allowed to happen the thing I dreaded most in life, which dumped me into a dark valley of death and betrayal.

Abandonment

But it didn't stop there. After betraying me by allowing Mom's cancer to happen in the first place, He abandoned me by not trying to make anything easier once we learned of her diagnosis. Everything was confusing to me, so much so that I couldn't point to one thing God was doing to help me. Then there was the physical toll: I was getting so sick and dropping weight like crazy. What could I count on Him for? Why couldn't Fred see these issues too?

God's abandonment prompted feelings of intense loneliness. And since He abandoned me, I abandoned Him, refusing to worship, read my Bible, or go to church. What was the point? He had caused all this distress in my life, and He obviously had no intention of intervening on my behalf.

In retrospect, I was frighteningly close to chucking everything, shutting off the Lord, and muddling through the rest of my life being ticked off at Him. For a few weeks I was angry enough to silently say, *I don't care, Lord. I just don't want anything to do with You anymore. You are a fraud.*

At the same time, though, I heard a voice within me shouting, *Don't do this, Brenda!* But I wasn't listening to that voice or His voice or anyone else's either. Even when Mom said something about the Lord being good, I would respond with a nasty comment like, "Yeah, that's why He allows cancer to happen!"

I couldn't see that He loved us, and I couldn't see any goodness in Him at all.

LACK OF CONTROL

As the tide of anger surged in, a tremendous fear washed in behind it. Control is supposed to stop fear, because if you have control, you can stop the things that are scaring you. But I had no control over the cancer. It was unbelievably frustrating that I couldn't get a handle on any part of the journey. My list of what I didn't want to have happen just happened anyway.

Though I knew God wasn't listening, I begged helplessly for each of them:

- *Don't make me have to take her into my house in Des Moines.*
- *Don't let me have to be with her when she has to leave her house for the last time.*
- *Lord, please, I don't want to be there when she says her last good-bye to Aunt Barbara.*
- *Please don't let me have to be with Mom when she dies.*

There was a whole list of things…and the Lord allowed every single one of them to happen. The final blow came at the last moment of Mom's life. Not only was I there when she died, but I was the one who gently rolled my comatose mother over to keep her comfortable, only to have her lung fluids shift, stopping her breathing on the spot.

Just like that. She was gone.

Of course, I had lost control of my emotions long before she passed away, prompting an oppressive barrage of panic attacks during the first several months of Mom's illness. I had never experienced a panic attack before, but as an RN, I knew a little about them. To be honest, I used to dismiss people with panic attacks as either crazy or weak minded, but I instantly changed my opinion as the first one crashed in on me shortly after Mom's diagnosis. I knew exactly what it was, and no two words could describe it better. Those panic attacks didn't just come and go, however. They came and stayed, settling in like a plague of locusts in my life, eating away everything in sight.

TIME-OUT

But…time-out for a moment. Why was Fred's response so different from mine? Losing Mom was torturously sad for both of us, no question. Yet as it turned out, my collapse wasn't about the traumatic loss of my relationship with Mom as much as it was about a flaw in my relationship with God. What happened was that I viewed Him through what I call "funny filters." Let me explain what funny—or flawed—filters are and where they come from.

Unintended journeys always take you where you don't want to go, often through no fault of your own. A cancer cell roots and reproduces, sometimes rapidly. A pornographic image roots and then escalates into addiction. Who's at fault? I could blame cancer on Satan, and you could certainly blame the pornographers for ensnaring your husband. But if you have a mind to, you can always trace the blame back to God too.

After all, God is omnipotent. That's why you're thinking, *God is supposed to be good. Why didn't He stop my wedding when He knew what was coming up ahead for me? God has the power to deliver my husband instantly from this sin, so why doesn't He do it? He's supposed to love me!* You know implicitly that He can stop anything that's out of your control, and He can easily rescue you from this journey. But He doesn't— or hasn't.

You may not pin the blame on God the first day, or the second day for that matter. But once the journey has dragged you through the mud for a while, it's easy to come around to that position.

Say, for example, your husband has waffled for a year about whether he really wants to be sexually pure or not. Because he hasn't dealt with the sin, it spreads. Now let's say you've recently caught your twelve-year-old masturbating to one of your husband's videos, and your fifteen-year-old daughter is pushing for shorter shorts, deeper necklines, and later curfews. You know that the generational grip of your husband's sin is tightening, and you're certain he has compromised the spiritual protection he is supposed to provide. Your husband is certainly at fault here, but you also know that the Lord could pick up the slack for him anytime He chose to.

That's when you're at a crossroads. When life doesn't turn out the way it's supposed to and you're getting frustrated, do you trust the Lord resolutely, or do you blame Him, stomping your feet in offense because He's not doing anything?

If your theological filters are true, you know implicitly that God is good, God loves you, and trials are simply trials. They're just part of the deal, and you wouldn't lay the blame for them on God in a million years.

But what if your filters are flawed…like mine were? Then you'd get offended and blame God.

So how did I get my funny filters? I got mine the hard way, as most of us do, born from the wounds of life. Life went out of kilter when my father died. I was just twenty years old at the time. Fred wrote this about Dad in *Every Man's Battle:*

> When I asked for Brenda's [hand] from my father-in-law, he was on his deathbed. He strengthened from time to time, but we both knew his time on earth was nearly over. I entered his hospital room, much stronger than he, but far more frightened. I knew how he loved his daughter. I knew how he once held her and let her cry when she came home with a squirrel-cut instead of a haircut. I knew how he proudly gave her a used red Chevy Nova as a gift. I knew how he used to swim way out into the ocean and let her sit on him like a raft, floating merrily. I knew how he had diligently raised her in purity, keeping her in church and away from ribald influences on her life.… When growing up, Brenda never feared anything because her dad was there. He never dishonored her, never shocked her, never frightened her, or let her down. (*Every Man's Battle,* 200, 202)

I was Dad's only daughter. He cherished me, and I felt the same way about him. He was practically perfect, and when he died, my grief was pure agony. I found the permanence of death completely breathtaking. My aching heart cried out to someone who was no longer there: *Let me hold your hand once more! Just let me hear you say "I love you" one more time. Let me have one more hug. Can you at least let me dream about you, so I can see you one more time?*

While his death was a stunning blow, the biggest wound came from the way we handled the situation before he died. My family never talked about the possibility that Dad would actually die. I just knew he would be healed if I prayed enough and fasted enough and if I refused to give in to the thought that he might die. As you might guess, his eventual death caused mass spiritual damage in me.

After that, something changed in my heart toward God. I wasn't conscious of the change, but that didn't matter. As far as I could see at the time, my family and I had done everything the Bible told us to do—prayed, fasted, anointed him with oil—and yet my dad died, in spite of our obedience.

End result: God couldn't be trusted.

At twenty, I was at the age when young adults begin to shift their dependency away from their parents and onto someone else, ideally the Lord. But how would that happen in light of this new information? Somewhere deep in my subconscious, it no longer made sense to dump my trustworthy parents in favor of God, so Mom took up the space in my life that was rightfully the Creator's. She was not God, but she was godly; I knew from experience that I could always count on her. I wasn't as sure about the Lord.

The inevitable happened when I found that my god—Mom—was about to be ripped out of my life by cancer. I took that very personally, and my rage and horror pushed my situation from sad to overwhelming. That's when I learned that a corner of my house was built on sand.

And now the deluge was washing it away.

SHIFTING FOCUS

If you feel like God hasn't come through for you and your family by delivering your husband from the fierce, pornographic squalls buffeting your lives, your trust in the Lord has likely taken a beating too. Perhaps old wounds have rushed to the surface, knocking your filters out of kilter. You may be offended by God big-time, and your frustration could be causing as much stress in your marriage as your husband's addiction.

But there's no shame in wounds. Was it child abuse? your dad's verbal battering? date rape? Perhaps you've become a great actress, hiding your pain from the world, but out here in the valley of wilderness, your haunting cry can no longer be silenced. Your husband's betrayal has those old feelings of defenselessness and fear bubbling over again as if all of it happened yesterday, and your hatred of men is a fiery, burning stew once more.

And how do you feel toward God? Betrayed? Probably so, since God didn't protect you back then and He hasn't bothered to stop your husband's sin and betrayals this time around either.

If you're offended with God, you're in good company. Jesus called John the Baptist the greatest man born of women (see Matthew 11:11), and God called Job "blameless and upright," "the greatest man among all the people of the East" (Job 1:3, 8), yet these two men, as great as they were, were both offended with God when their lives didn't meet their expectations. In the next chapter, we'll take a closer look at their stories and see how the Lord responded to them as they plunged headlong into their unintended journeys.

3

Clearing Your Filters

As the greatest man born among women, it is only fitting that John the Baptist experienced one of the greatest moments of history:

> The next day John saw Jesus coming toward him and said, "Look, the Lamb of God, who takes away the sin of the world! This is the one I meant when I said, 'A man who comes after me has surpassed me because he was before me.' I myself did not know him, but the reason I came baptizing with water was that he might be revealed to Israel."
>
> Then John gave this testimony: "I saw the Spirit come down from heaven as a dove and remain on him. I would not have known him, except that the one who sent me to baptize with water told me, 'The man on whom you see the Spirit come down and remain is he who will baptize with the Holy Spirit.' I have seen and I testify that this is the Son of God." (John 1:29–34)

What a culmination of destiny in this young man's life! He had to be aware of what the angel had prophesied to his father, Zechariah—

that John would prepare the way for the Messiah and "bring back" the people of Israel "to the wisdom of the righteous" (Luke 1:13–17).

I can also imagine that there was a moment when John was poring over the scrolls of Isaiah and a verse popped off the page like a spark from a blaze, burning a hole in his heart:

> A voice of one calling:
> "In the desert prepare
>   the way for the LORD;
> make straight in the wilderness
>   a highway for our God." (Isaiah 40:3)

John must have thought, *Whoa, that's me! I'm that man. I'm that voice!*

Can you imagine the responsibility of that call? John's expressed purpose in life was to prepare the way for the Messiah, the Lion of Judah, the Balm of Gilead, the Promised One that his people had been longing for throughout the millennia. But John had carried this responsibility well, and now with Jesus's commissioning behind him, John's heart was completely at rest.

In John's ministry and life, everything unfolded just as his study of the sacred scrolls as a young man led him to expect. He had prepared the way for his Lord, and now the Messiah was boldly preaching and advancing His public ministry in great power. To John, everything seemed to be lining up exactly as it should, as this passage indicates:

> After this, Jesus and his disciples went out into the Judean coun-
> tryside, where he spent some time with them, and baptized.
> Now John also was baptizing at Aenon near Salim, because there
> was plenty of water, and people were constantly coming to be
> baptized.… An argument developed between some of John's dis-

ciples and a certain Jew over the matter of ceremonial washing. They came to John and said to him, "Rabbi, that man who was with you on the other side of the Jordan—the one you testified about—well, he is baptizing, and everyone is going to him."

To this John replied, "A man can receive only what is given him from heaven. You yourselves can testify that I said, 'I am not the Christ but am sent ahead of him.' The bride belongs to the bridegroom. The friend who attends the bridegroom waits and listens for him, and is full of joy when he hears the bridegroom's voice. That joy is mine, and it is now complete. He must become greater; I must become less." (John 3:22–30)

A GREAT ATTITUDE

With his humility and maturity, John stood head and shoulders above the rest. He had such a tremendous walk with God that he was willing to let Jesus have the headlines. But that didn't mean John quit being John—it was still his destiny to exhort others to repentance, even the rich and powerful of his day. One of those rich and powerful people was Herod the tetrarch, a royal governor installed by Rome. When John the Baptist called out Herod for marrying his brother's wife, the king didn't appreciate it at all. Neither did his new wife, Herodias, who was so furious she wanted John killed. Herod chose instead to bind John and toss him into prison.

Suddenly, John's life wasn't going as he expected, and in his mind, events were no longer lining up with what he knew about God and the Messiah from the scrolls. We've already seen what that kind of disappointment did in my life. After praying for twenty-four long years against cancer, I expected I'd never see this nasty disease up close again. When the deadly sickness showed up anyway, confusion set in, raising all kinds of questions in me about God's integrity and kindness.

Did John's great courage and peerless maturity make a difference in his case? Not really, which is somewhat comforting to folks like me. Before long, John was frustrated and deeply confused. Here's how Matthew recounted the story:

> Now it came to pass, when Jesus finished commanding His twelve disciples, that He departed from there to teach and to preach in their cities. And when John had heard in prison about the works of Christ, *he sent two of his disciples and said to Him, "Are You the Coming One, or do we look for another?"* (Matthew 11:1–3, NKJV)

What an odd question for John to ask! John had already answered that question many times himself. With his own eyes he had seen the Spirit settle on Jesus like a dove, and by now a constant stream of astonishing, miraculous news was pouring in daily from the Judean countryside. The Christ's supernatural power and grace had been anticipated by Isaiah, and John saw their fulfillment in Jesus. So why was John asking whether Jesus was "the Coming One"?

Now, if you think John's question was odd, get a load of the Lord's response to him:

> Jesus answered and said to them, "Go and tell John the things which you hear and see: The blind see and the lame walk; the lepers are cleansed and the deaf hear; the dead are raised up and the poor have the gospel preached to them. *And blessed is he who is not offended because of Me.*" (Matthew 11:4–6, NKJV)

Blessed is he who is not offended? Why did Christ add *that* thought? At first blush, that response was just as unusual as John's original question—sure, John was confused, but how could this remarkably humble and powerful prophet possibly get offended by his Messiah? They might as well have been speaking in code to each other, but Jesus—being who He was—understood the context of John's question, which was borne out of a wounded and suffering spirit.

You see, it's not that there wasn't ample proof everywhere that Jesus was the true Messiah. The problem was that none of it was happening anywhere near John, so when John's friends brought his question to Jesus, the Lord knew what John was really saying, which was something like this: *Listen, Jesus, I called You the Lamb of God, and You didn't deny it. Did I get suckered? Are You the One or not, because some things have happened to me that I wasn't expecting—like getting tossed into prison.*

John felt that the Messiah had abandoned him, just as I felt when He allowed Mom to get cancer after my twenty-four years of prayer. What exactly was John thinking about his predicament? The Bible doesn't tell us directly, but it's pretty easy to guess what was stirring in his mind.

Sitting in his dank cell, John was likely comparing his situation to Elijah's, who, in obedience to God, had confronted the evil rulers of his era—sullen, pouty Ahab and his seductive wife, Jezebel. At one point, she became so angry with Elijah that she swore by her gods to kill him by the next evening.

So what did Elijah receive from God in return for his obedience?

The ability to perform eye-popping miracles. The ravens fed him meat and bread daily for a year as he hid from Jezebel. When Elijah declared there would be no rain until he said so, the land was parched. When Elijah later declared that rain would fall, the water came down in buckets. He called down the fire of God in his battle with the prophets of Baal and Asherah. After outrunning Ahab's chariot from Mount Carmel to Jezreel, he traveled forty days and forty nights to Mount Horeb on the strength of two simple, angelic meals.

John had to be expecting nothing less from God when he confronted his own evil king and queen. So what did he receive in return for his obedience to God?

A brutal, open-ended prison sentence.

John was on an unintended journey if I ever saw one. Miracles were blossoming everywhere as spiritual revival spread across the hills of Judea, and as God's personal messenger to prepare His Son's way on earth, John had likely dreamed of playing a significant role in those miraculous times. How could the Messiah leave him out? I can just imagine what the Enemy was whispering in his ear as he rotted in that prison cell. *Oh yeah, God's really moving out there, but He's not moving in your life, pal. You got Him started in ministry, and now He's abandoned you. Some Messiah He's turned out to be!*

This is where John's filters probably began to skew and get funny, but it wasn't enough to throw him completely into confusion. After all, John had to know that he was not the first prophet in history to be imprisoned unfairly. That dreamer Joseph probably came quickly to his mind, and Jeremiah had spent some time in jail as well. Prophets go to prison sometimes. So why did John feel that prison was out of line for him?

Precisely because he was living in the days of Messiah. In John's mind, he had a legitimate expectation of freedom in this hour, as Isaiah had suggested that faithful men would not languish in dungeons during the days of Jesus. The scrolls couldn't have been clearer:

> The Spirit of the Sovereign LORD is on me, because the LORD has anointed me to preach good news to the poor. He has sent me to bind up the brokenhearted, *to proclaim freedom for the captives and release from darkness for the prisoners.* (Isaiah 61:1)

John was about to step into the same trap I fell into—that of taking offense with God when your circumstances don't line up with what you know about Him—but there is an important difference between our stories that you need to keep in mind. I took offense with God when bad things began happening all around me. John's problem was that good things were happening in everyone's life but his own. Paraphrasing a little, Jesus warned John of this trap when He said, *And blessed is he who is not offended because of Me—and all that I'm doing in the others around you.*

Testimonies aren't always fuel for faith if you're tossing your own dashed expectations into the mix, are they? Let's say your support group has been praying for breakthroughs in the lives of your husbands for a solid six months, and then let's say that the husbands of your three closest friends in that group are now walking free of their sin, pure as freshly fallen snow. What happens when your husband admits to you that he's still masturbating twice a week? Good things are happening in every family but your own, and it's like the Enemy of your soul is perched on your shoulder and whispering, *If God were good, He'd quit playing games with your life while He's out delivering everyone else except your husband.*

The good news is that you don't have to give in to that offense. You can choose to believe that God is loving and good at all times, no matter what your circumstances are, no matter how deeply your husband has betrayed you with his sexual sin. You can choose to live above your stark circumstances, far out of earshot of your Enemy. Do so, and you'll be blessed immeasurably.

The word Jesus used for "blessed" was also used in ancient Grecian literature to describe the emotional state of the Greek gods—joyous, content, happy, and well-adjusted. They were joyous and contented because they lived above the fray on earth, totally immune to its vagaries and churning chaos.

The Greek gods were myths, but my God isn't, and neither is that place of emotional blessing that those "deities" supposedly lived in. Jesus was offering that place—that blessing—to John if he would just resist offense. It was certainly possible to do it. Contrast John's behavior to that of Paul and Silas, who were also tossed into prison. These two captives chose to live free inside prison, joyous enough to worship openly and to bless those in captivity with them, giving them all the freedom to live in Christ (see Acts 16:22–34).

Fred had found that place too. He became like Paul and Silas in the midst of my unintended journey, blessing everyone around him and being such an encouragement to our children. Even as he prayed in desperation for Mom's life, he lived in a blessed realm that I didn't understand at the time. As I said earlier, there was nothing about the way Mom's terminal situation was playing out that confused Fred in the least, because nothing about the harsh reality of Mom's diagnosis was out of line with Fred's theological filters. God was good, and Fred knew that God loved him—and Mom. The trials and tribulations had nothing to do with God's steadfast love.

While Fred did not choose to take offense at God when we learned she had just months to live, I chose a different path, questioning whether God loved me or even cared about me. But Jesus wants you to know that when it comes to your unintended journey, you need to leave any offense in your spirit at the door so that you may receive His great blessing, which can restore your heart in the midst of your trial and help you begin to bless others around you on your journey.

GATHERING COURAGE

I certainly needed that overflow of God's blessing from Fred. He urged me to stretch and enjoy my last days with Mom. "We only have a few more months to enjoy all of who she is," he said. "Once those days are gone, they will be gone. Help me live them out with you."

Fred uttered those words repeatedly at a time when I was avoiding

Mom so I wouldn't have to deal with the pain of watching her slowly waste away. Happily, with God's help through Scripture, I began seeing things as Fred did, which allowed me to stretch a little, in spite of my pain. I don't know how I could have lived with myself if I'd avoided Mom completely during her year of sickness. Fred saved me from that, but he also did something far greater.

Watching Fred, I began to realize that a miraculous escape from my unintended journey wasn't necessarily the only ticket out of my pain and chaos. I saw that there was a place in God, above my trials and tribulations, where I could go to be joyous, content, happy, and well-adjusted all the time, in spite of the trauma. And through his influence, my hope was stirred.

When Fred speaks to men about sexual purity, he talks of a place in God where the male mind has been so transformed by God's truth that the temptation to sin sexually virtually dies. Fred knows that place exists because he lives there. Hearing about that place gives men hope.

In a similar way, Fred gave me hope for *my* future. He knew of a place of blessing in God—that place above the circumstances—because he obviously lived there. It helped me understand what Jesus was telling John: that the Father promises each of us a joy that's immune to our circumstances when we surrender our hearts and resist this offense in God.

That's the hope I want to offer you. Through His promises, I found that place myself, even while I was still in the midst of my trial. And the truth is, you can find that place too, right now. If there is anything I've learned from life on this earth, it is this: pain is pain. It doesn't matter whether your trial involves deep grief, tragic violence, a severe accident, or your husband's sexual sin.

But I've also learned that no matter what the trauma, we have the same clear choice between life and death: *will we surrender our hearts and resist being offended by God?*

In the following section, Fred expands upon what he taught me.

FROM FRED

How do you make the choice to avoid taking offense at God and live in the blessing that Jesus promised you? How do you keep the right perspective in the midst of trial and tribulation? Start by keeping these fundamental truths in mind:

1. God is good at all times. He'll never change.
2. God is your precious Father, and you're the apple of His eye. He will complete what He has authored in you, and He'll never love anyone more than He loves you.
3. Christ overcame the world, but you'll still have trials and tribulations because a third-party intruder (Satan) retains temporary dominion on earth.

Trusting completely in God's goodness and love allows you to live above the fray and thrive in the midst of unintended journeys. In other words, you choose to avoid offense with God when you take a stand on the first two of these fundamental truths and hold on to them with all of your heart, mind, soul, and spirit: *Your Word says You are good, and Your Word says You love me with an everlasting love. Lord, I won't let go of these truths no matter what I see around me.*

Yet unless you also understand the third fundamental truth inside and out, you won't be able to stand there long, as your heaviest troubles will trip you up. As you know, Brenda found that out the hard way. When God didn't jump through Brenda's hoops the way she expected, the unfolding, painful trauma became her "evidence" that God was the cruel, heartless perpetrator of it all. Understanding the true source of your trials and tribulations will keep you from misinterpreting God's character by your difficult circumstances.

It's easy to make this mistake, though. Take Job. He was a well-respected patriarch with seven sons and three daughters, sheep, camels, and oxen by the thousands, and very wealthy. He trusted in God, but the devil was allowed to inflict terrible things on him: the loss of his family, all his livestock, and all his possessions. At first, Job thought God caused the problems (see Job 19:1–12), not realizing that the devil was behind his afflictions. As I said, blaming God for our trials is where our filters get funny. Interpreting God by our circumstances is a natural trap hidden beneath one of the great philosophical dilemmas of Western Christianity: if God is all-loving and all-powerful, why do the innocent suffer in this world? Today, many people answer this question by saying, "Since innocent people do suffer, God cannot be all-loving or all-powerful. If He were, He would show His love and His power by eliminating suffering and caring adequately for His creation." To come to this conclusion, people must make the same three assumptions made by most philosophers throughout the ages:

1. God is not almighty, and therefore, He can't protect the innocent from suffering.
2. God has a dark streak, a "demonic" element to His being, and that's why the innocent suffer.
3. Humans can be innocent enough to preclude suffering in their lives.

Of course, to the ancient Jews, it was indisputable that God was almighty, perfectly just, and that no human was wholly innocent in God's sight. Since in their minds there were only two parties involved in this debate—God and man—and since God was almighty and completely good, they were left with only one possible conclusion: if an "innocent" man was suffering, it had to be his own fault. No man was as innocent as he seemed, and if you could only see into the secret corners of the sufferer's life, you would surely find that the whole debate had been a mirage in the first place—the "innocent" one was actually getting exactly what he deserved from God's hand.

Of course, this could only mean one thing from a theological perspective: the level of one's suffering was a perfect barometer of one's guilt before God—which was what Job and his friends believed. When Job's world came crashing down around him, Job's friends naturally assumed he'd done something horrible. And before his unintended journey, Job would have wholeheartedly agreed with their thinking. The theology seemed self-evident to all of them.

But to Job, it was now disorienting, because his circumstances no longer matched up with what he knew about God. Job was innocent, and he knew it. Why would God disappear on him and leave him to writhe alone except for a few well-meaning friends who stuck around to jab at the integrity of his heart?

Job *knew* that his high moral character and purity in heart and spirit should have set him above such "punishment." He *didn't* have a secret sin, which left him certain that even those who were innocent before God could fall victim to disaster. As he wrestled to come to grips with this shocking new truth, he was also left struggling with an even bigger issue: if he was suffering through no fault of his own, what did that say about God's character?

It's right here at this question where we can slip up and begin to interpret God by our circumstances, and it was Job's struggle over this question that made his story relevant to our particular family situation. We, too, had someone with high moral character—Gwen—who was suffering horribly through no fault of her own. Brenda, too, was left writhing alone with her questions after God seemed to disappear on her. Brenda had never strayed from God's ways and had prayed against cancer for twenty-four years. Since she *knew* she'd done nothing wrong, God's character had to be off-kilter, right? Job's reasoning had drifted in the same direction. Since his suffering didn't result from his own secret sin, there had to be a flaw in God. What could it be?

Fortunately, the only flaw here is in their reasoning, and the missing piece in their logic completely resolves the dilemma: *the relationship between God and man is not exclusive and closed.* In other words, when it comes to the suffering of the innocent, there aren't just two parties involved, as supposed by the ancient Jews and current philosophers. And we also aren't limited by only two positions to choose from: *God is sadistic* or *the sufferer has secret sin.*

You see, there is a third-party intruder out there, a great Adversary who is fixed on ruining God's plan for His creation by alienating us from our Creator in an irreconcilable way. While this is hardly news to a Christian, it might as well be when it comes to our unintended journeys. In our panic and despair, all we can see is our own pain and our own situation. We forget all about the Enemy and his third-party impact, and we're right back to "only God and me" in the equation.

Once there, it's inevitable that you're soon confused, like Job. You know that the Lord is all-powerful, so no one can stop Him. You know that He's all-loving and that you are His crying, desperate child. So where is His help? What's wrong with Him?

There's nothing wrong with God. There's just more to it than that. Your relationship with Him is not exclusive and closed, remember? There is a third party involved, and that complicates things.

In the story of Job, for instance, the Enemy attacked the intimate relationship between God and His godly friend to alienate one from the other. When God proclaimed Job's great righteousness, the devil sneered and denounced Job's obedience as the worst kind of sin because Job's motives were utterly selfish. The Accuser claimed that Job was only righteous because he believed it led to blessing, and that if the link between righteousness and blessing were broken, Job would be exposed as the duplicitous phony he really was.

How would God respond to this accusation? What options were open to Him? When I first read the following two paragraphs in the study notes of my Bible, my soul was blasted with light. I would never again think the same way about my difficult circumstances:

> It is the adversary's ultimate challenge. For if godliness…can be
> shown to be the worst of all sins, then a chasm of alienation

stands between them that cannot be bridged. Then even
redemption is unthinkable, for the godliest of men will be
shown to be the most ungodly. God's whole enterprise in
creation and redemption will be shown to be radically flawed,
and God can only sweep it all away in awful judgment.

*The accusation, once raised, cannot be removed, even by
destroying the accuser.* So God lets the adversary have his way
with Job (within specified limits) so that [*if* Job continues in
obedience] God and the righteous Job may be vindicated and
the great accuser silenced. Thus comes the anguish of Job…
[but] he will not curse God. In fact, what pains him most is
God's apparent alienation from him. (The NIV Study Bible,
Zondervan, 731–32, emphasis added)

That italicized line left me breathless. For the first time, I understood that although almighty God is omnipotent, in some cases He
must lay aside His power to defend His just character and to vindicate
us before all creation. God's power would have done no good here…
and even destroying Satan wouldn't have removed the accusation. Because of God's perfect justice, there was no choice but to let some
tragedies play out in Job's life in order to silence Satan and remove that
accusation from heaven, and God was counting on Job's trust in Him
to keep any alienation at bay.

That puts every trial we face in a whole new light. The suffering of
the godly is the result of the war in heaven between the Enemy and
God, the direct or collateral damage crashing into our lives from the
titanic spiritual struggle of the ages, and there's a lot more going on out
there than we realize. Reaching this conclusion was a huge turning
point for me, and I hope it is for you. This is the bottom line: *God may
be omnipotent, but that doesn't mean He can, will, or should eliminate
every unintended journey of your life.* As He fights for you and your rela-

tionship together, He must be true to *every* aspect of His nature and character, not just His omnipotence. Your role in the battle is to trust His character no matter how things look out there.

Understanding this can make all the difference in how you view God and make sense of the pain in your life. Without this understanding, there's no way to avoid taking offense at God or to live in the blessing Jesus wants to give you, because you'll keep fighting with Him in your heart, questioning His character and blaming Him for not using His omnipotence on your behalf.

But you *can* keep from taking offense—misinterpreting God by your circumstances—if you understand the true source of the trials. First, you live in a fallen world with inescapable curses brought about by human sin, and you certainly can't blame God for any of those troubles. Second, a third-party intruder is responsible for the rest of your trials and tribulations, the result of the cosmic war that he's declared against the Most High. In other words, trials and tribulations are just part of the deal down here. Since God bears no blame for them, you can't interpret His character through them. God is implicitly good, and trials are simply trials. That's it.

Because I've embraced this truth about difficult circumstances, my attitude following Gwen's diagnosis went something like this: *God, I can't figure this all out and it hurts like crazy, but I trust You. I refuse to interpret You by my circumstances, and I am not going to backslide over a mystery. Your Word says You are good. I'm taking my stand right there, and I will not let go of it.*

I firmly believe that if you take the same stand, you will survive any unintended journey. And more than survive—you can thrive. He loves you, and you are the apple of His eye, no matter what you see around you. He's encouraging you to turn back to Him, and to implicitly trust His love and goodness.

And He will pursue you until you do.

4

Resurrecting Your Heart

FROM BRENDA

God zealously pursues us in the midst of our unintended journeys. What motivates His heart on these journeys of ours? What does He dream of seeing in us on the other end?

To help you understand, it would be instructive to turn to the story about Martha and Mary and the resurrection of Lazarus. We're used to seeing Martha as the offended party, but if you read between the lines, you'll find that Mary, too, can claim membership in the Offended Hearts Club Band. This is how her story begins:

> On his arrival, Jesus found that Lazarus had already been in the tomb for four days. Bethany was less than two miles from Jerusalem, and many Jews had come to Martha and Mary to comfort them in the loss of their brother. When Martha heard that Jesus was coming, she went out to meet him, but Mary stayed at home. (John 11:17–20)

Mary stayed at home? How can that be?

Mary was no ordinary follower of Jesus. She lived in the village of Bethany with her brother Lazarus and her sister Martha, and they were some of the closest friends that Jesus had. While Jesus had no place of His own to lay His head, you could make a strong biblical case for calling Bethany His home base and the house belonging to Mary's family His headquarters. When Jesus was "home," you couldn't pry Mary away from His feet with a crowbar, as this passage indicates:

> [Martha] had a sister called Mary, who sat at the Lord's feet listening to what he said. But Martha was distracted by all the preparations that had to be made. She came to him and asked, "Lord, don't you care that my sister has left me to do the work by myself? Tell her to help me!"
>
> "Martha, Martha," the Lord answered, "you are worried and upset about many things, but only one thing is needed. Mary has chosen what is better, and it will not be taken away from her." (Luke 10:39–42)

But Mary didn't just love His teaching. She loved *Him,* and she was a passionate worshiper of His beauty and grace in her life:

> Six days before the Passover, Jesus arrived at Bethany.... Here a dinner was given in Jesus' honor.... Then Mary took about a pint of pure nard, an expensive perfume; she poured it on Jesus' feet and wiped his feet with her hair. And the house was filled with the fragrance of the perfume. (John 12:1–3)

Mary loved Jesus like crazy, pouring out a year's wages worth of aromatic nard—an essential oil much like an expensive perfume—over Jesus's dusty feet and tossing her reputation to the winds in an extravagant, shocking display of worship.

Just as shocking was Mary's decision to dry Jesus's feet with her hair. It was scandalous for a woman to drop her hair in public in that culture, and even today an orthodox Jewish woman will only release her gathered hair in the presence of her husband and only in their bed-chamber. Yet Mary was so overwhelmed with gratitude and affection for Jesus that she wiped His feet with her long tresses.

That's our Mary. *But Mary stayed home.* That just doesn't make sense! What could possibly keep this passionate follower at home when Jesus was in the vicinity? Check out why Jesus was heading into town in the first place:

> Now a man named Lazarus was sick....
>
> When he heard this, Jesus said, "This sickness will not end in death. No, it is for God's glory so that God's Son may be glorified through it." Jesus loved Martha and her sister and Lazarus. Yet when he heard that Lazarus was sick, he stayed where he was two more days. (John 11:1, 4–6)

By the time Jesus reached Bethany, Lazarus had already been dead in the tomb for four days! Martha, the distracted, busy sister, rushed out to meet Jesus, but Mary stayed home. Martha's opening shot offers us a clue about why:

> "Lord," Martha said to Jesus, "if you had been here, my brother would not have died." (John 11:21)

Is it possible that Mary was offended? Sounds like it. Jesus seemingly ignored her urgent plea, dawdling and taking His time getting to Bethany. And now her brother lay decomposing in a wormy tomb outside town. Jesus spoke of love incessantly, yet His actions contradicted everything she'd learned about love while sitting at His feet.

Mary had been certain that Jesus would hightail it to Bethany the moment He heard about Lazarus's illness, but instead He poked along heartlessly for two whole days. Something had happened in Mary's heart, and she was no longer pursuing Him the way she had before. Wounded and disoriented by His delay, Mary was unmoved by the fact that He was nearby. She stayed where she was, thinking, *Lord, if You would have just been here! Where were You?*

When we stop pursuing God, Jesus never leaves it there. Instead, He steps it up a notch on His end, pursuing us passionately in two distinct ways:

- through direct, personal invitations
- through loving silence and delays

And in fact, both of these display His love beautifully.

HIS PERSONAL PURSUIT OF YOU

Jesus wasn't about to leave His relationship with Mary in her hands alone. When Mary didn't come out to greet Him, Jesus wasn't offended in return. Instead, He responded by pursuing her. He wanted her to know that He understood her feelings about the delay. He invited her to pour out her heart at His feet once more, so that they might be one again:

> And after [Martha] had said this, she went back and called her sister Mary aside. "The Teacher is here," she said, "and is asking for you." (John 11:28)

His kind invitation tugged at her heart, giving her the courage to fall at His feet in tears and declare what was weighing on her mind:

> When Mary heard this, she got up quickly and went to him.... When Mary reached the place where Jesus was and saw him, she

fell at his feet and said, "Lord, if you had been here, my brother would not have died." (John 11:29, 32)

As it was with Mary, your first step in restoring your heart on an unintended journey will be responding passionately to His personal pursuit of you. Mary did not delay an instant, and we can learn from that example.

Jesus loves you as much as He loved Mary, so He will pursue you with a personal invitation to fully trust Him again. Remember, He asked to speak with Mary, and He'll ask to speak with you too. When He calls, run to where He is and pour out your heart. I wished I'd done the same following Mom's diagnosis.

It's not that I missed His call. I heard His invitation loud and clear, but I was too confused to respond to Him at that time. Do you feel that way? If so, remember this: No matter how far you've withdrawn from Him, He still sees you. He still loves you. He's not ashamed to call you His, and He's not even ashamed to get down on one knee to offer you His engraved invitation, through one of your sisters if that's what it takes.

The invitation He gave me came through a friend I'll call Sandy, who regularly prays for our ministry:

While praying, I saw you, Brenda, as a little girl, walking between your father (on the right) and your mother (on the left), one on each side holding your hand. You were so happy, just laughing and giggling. I could tell you felt very safe and secure in the protection and love that surrounded you. In time, Gwen released your hand and moved to the other side with your dad, and Fred took your empty hand in marriage.

I could still see you dwelling in their protection, but soon it was just Fred and Gwen holding your hands. Though you were hurt deeply by the loss of your father, you continued living happily in the shelter and love you received from Fred and your mother.

The scene then switched to the present. As Gwen's hand began to slip slowly out of yours, Jesus Himself reached out for your right hand. You kept grasping for your Mom's hand, for that safe place you had always known, but the Lord wants you to know that He's desired to be the one holding your hand for some time now. He promises that if you would reach out and hold His hand directly, you will learn an unshakable dependence on Him that you have never fully realized before. This will also drive you to a higher level of prayer to which you have been called but in which you have not walked consistently, a level that is beyond anything you've known or understood before.

How could an invitation be this accurate and so generous unless it came from Jesus's personal pursuit of my heart? What Sandy said was so tender, so passionate that it bordered on the romantic.

But I still didn't budge. To tell you the truth, He'd already been offering me this exact invitation during my own prayer times for a number of weeks. Somehow I knew He wanted me to take His hand, but I found it virtually impossible to let go of Mom's hand, in spite of His gentle pursuit. To let go of her hand felt more like I was cutting off my own—with a dull, serrated blade to boot.

HIS PERSONAL PURSUIT IN SILENCE OR DELAYS

When you simply can't respond to a direct, personal, loving invitation, the Lord is undeterred. He's creative. He'll simply shift course and pursue you another way, often through periods of silence or delays. Let me assure you that when you're careening through an unintended journey and you're feeling like you're not hearing anything from the Lord, He's still in hot pursuit of your heart.

Silence may be the perfect means of getting through to you, given the circumstances. You're not convinced? Well, let me prove it.

When my older son, Jasen, was in his final year of college, he became interested in a lovely young woman named Rose, who worked at our church. As is often the case with guys, Jasen didn't want to blow the cover on his interest in Rose unless he received reciprocal signs of interest. But when Jasen put some tentative feelers out there, Rose didn't respond. Jasen heard nothing but silence.

It wasn't that Rose had no interest in my son; actually, she was quite enamored with Jasen. It's just that Rose had some firm views on what's right and wrong in dating relationships. She felt that when dating, it's best for the guy to be the open pursuer since, after all, he's supposed to be the spiritual leader. She also believed that a good, hearty pursuit was important for the male heart.

She knew that Jasen wanted to feel good and secure as he approached this new relationship, but because of her higher motives, Rose couldn't afford to worry about whether he felt good as he approached her. She was after his greatest good, which forced her to stand by lovingly in silence, playing hard to get for a while. Rose wanted to make sure Jasen's interest in her grew from the passions of his heart. She wanted to know that my son was pursuing her for the right reasons—not because she was making it easy for him.

How long could she—should she—hold out? She wasn't sure, but I've never seen a girl throw so much smoke in all my life. She even had Fred fooled, which is saying something.

Jasen approached her a number of times to chat and thought up innocuous reasons to e-mail her. He called her cell phone regularly to see how she was doing, and he even joined her singles' group at church, in spite of the half-hour drive from Iowa State University every Thursday night. Rose was extremely outgoing and friendly to Jasen, just as she was to all her other friends in the group. But as for sending out vibes that she hoped Jasen might become something more than that…forget about it.

So Jasen backed off and shifted into neutral for a while. Since she was showing no signs of interest in him, he figured she really wasn't into him. He kept up the impromptu chats and e-mails because of their budding friendship, but he pulled back on his thoughts of asking her out on a date until he could come up with a Plan B.

In the meantime, though, Rose was dying inside. In fact, one day Fred stopped by our church—she was the receptionist—and chatted with Rose. We found out later that after Fred left, Rose ran to our pastor, pointed at Fred through the window, and burst into tears, confiding in him, "I'm in love with that man's son, and I can't let him know it!"

We never heard about this until long after Jasen and Rose became an item, because at the time, Rose was certain that silence—or passivity—was her best means of drawing Jason in. How she held out under that emotional pressure, I'll never know. In the end, Jasen threw caution to the wind and courageously put his cards on the table, figuring it was better to get slapped down now and get on with life than to forever sit at the side of the road stuck in neutral. Once he announced his intentions to woo her heart, starting with an invitation to dinner, she smiled as if to say, *Game on.* Within seven months, they were pledging their love to each other "until death do we part," and we had gained an incredible daughter-in-law.

So did you catch the connection? I'd have bet the farm that Rose didn't care a fig about Jasen back in the early days. And yet she was passionately interested in him. Trouble was, because of her sacrificial motivation, she could not express that interest, at least not after Jasen's first overtures. Remaining silent carried some risk, because Jasen was left alone to wrestle with confusion for a while. But she believed the risk would be worth it, as this was the only way to ensure Jasen entered the relationship with a completely surrendered heart.

It was the same way with Jesus and me. When it came to Mom's cancer, I wanted her healed immediately, and I was only concerned with feeling good again in my circle of relationships. But Jesus had different motives. He cared a lot more about my greatest good than He did about my feeling good.

He wasn't silent because He was disinterested in me, as it appeared on the surface. He was extremely interested in everything that happened to me on my unintended journey. He simply had no other way to pursue me than to stand by lovingly in silence until my heart was ready and in the right place for Him.

THE WAY GOD OPERATES

God has two primary motivations in His relationship with us:

1. His glory
2. our greatest good

That's how God operates on these painful journeys. As to how He pursues you, sometimes you'll find an engraved personal invitation hitting your mailbox; other times you'll detect deafening silence. In either case, His motivations are true and His love is relentless. You must understand this and accept that He may pursue you at times in silence.

Otherwise, you'll become offended with Him.

You must also accept that when He finally does move, His first priority is to deal with the underlying attitudes within your heart, not to change your situation. When you cry out, *God, let me out of here!* God might whisper back lovingly, *You must grow first.*

If you're going through a hard time and God seems awfully quiet, remember this—God is never disconnected. God loves you and is moved by your situation, weeping with you just as He wept with Mary on the road outside Bethany. But that same love and His view of the big picture may prompt Him to wait, just as He did with Lazarus.

In every situation, God's heart is motivated by your greatest good. But let's not forget that He has His glory in mind too. That's one reason He waits until your situation is beyond human remedy—because that simultaneously brings about your greatest good *and* His greatest glory.

Consider the resurrection of Lazarus. Mary wanted Jesus to rush over and heal him on the spot before her brother died. But let's face it— in that part of the world at that particular moment in history, Jesus's healing of the sick had become old news, so common that Mary felt she could count on it at the asking.

But resurrecting a decomposing body that reeked after four days of death? Now that was something new, which put a whole new spin on why Jesus chose to tarry on the road for a couple of days. He deferred His arrival "for God's glory so that God's Son may be glorified through it" (John 11:4).

You may want God to move in before your situation gets too bad, but God knows that only decomposition—physical or spiritual—can bring you to the point where you'll admit, *Okay, what's happening to me is beyond human remedy. There's no way I can fix or control it.* At that point, He is all that's left to you. Jesus is your only option. This brings Him glory, and this also brings Him your heart in complete surrender.

Now, let's return to the subject of my mom. While God's motivations were true, mine were askew. I was only motivated to avoid pain. As much as I loved Mom, I wanted her cancer out of my universe, and I was running from anything that had to do with her condition, avoiding hospice nurses and hiding handicapped permits and oxygen tanks— you name it.

But guess what I learned? I couldn't control Mom's cancer, and I couldn't run away from it, no matter how fast or how far I ran. Misdirected by my funny filters, I then couldn't respond to God's direct pursuit either. So He simply stepped back lovingly to pursue me in another way, waiting until my situation decomposed enough for me to see what He already knew—that Mom's terminal disease was beyond human remedy. God had to let my world fall apart before He could help me, just as He did with Mary's in Bethany.

A few weeks after my weekend at Stoney Creek Inn, the following question crystallized deep within my heart: *Should I give up my plans and throw myself at His feet, like Mary did outside Bethany, or should I withdraw from Him forever?*

I was at the point of decision.

I told myself firmly, *You're either going to stay like this, or you're going to have to grow.* Speaking this way to myself was an unusual pattern for me. Normally, when faced with stress or confrontation, I have a simple motto: When the going gets tough, grab a novel and curl up on the couch!

There would be no couch on this occasion, however. Something had grabbed me by the throat, and I was scared. Things had decomposed too far, and I knew I was at a turning point in my life. As I counted the costs, I was thinking, *If I truly am a Christian, and if I am going to serve the Lord with any honesty, I must be willing to give Him everything, including Mom and the outcome of her cancer. I must give Him every other member of my family too, even if I live to be one hundred years of age and have to watch Fred and every one of my children die brutally by cancer, one by one. I have to give Him everything I hold dear, with no strings attached.*

The moment finally came at home one afternoon about a month after my stay at Stoney Creek Inn, when I prayed these words with all my heart: *All right, Lord, I once made a choice to stop trusting You. Now I'm going to begin to trust You again, and I'm going to begin to trust that Your Word is true and right for me. I will believe all that You say, all Your words, and I'm going to believe them as true. I will trust You for every single day and for everything that comes my way.* Letting go of Mom's hand, so to speak, I placed my hand firmly in His.

Finally, I was free.

Finally, He was free to move.

In one sense, this decision marked the end of my journey. I felt such relief as I let go of my anger and frustration and all the dark feelings bottled up within my heart. I told the Lord, *I'm done. I'll take my hands off. It is all Yours, Lord!*

NEVER A DOUBT

But in another sense, I found that my journey was just beginning, similar to the way we experience salvation. Salvation happens at a single point in time, and so did my decision to begin trusting the Lord. You give the Lord your heart, and His new life surges through you. You are born again, and from that moment on, your eternal destiny is secure.

But it's also true that your salvation is "worked out" over time. In other words, while you may *be* a Christian, you may not be *acting* like one in the least. Fred was saved one gorgeous California evening in May, and I met him one blustery morning in Iowa the following February. Yet he was still getting drunk during most of those months. R-rated movies were still his entertainment of choice, and porn still had its hooks set deeply in him.

Salvation was Fred's priceless ticket to paradise, no question. But in another sense, that ticket was nothing more than his registration into obedience school. The apostle Paul talked about this process in the New Testament:

> My dear ones, as you have always obeyed [my suggestions], so
> now, not only [with the enthusiasm you would show] in my pres-

ence but much more because I am absent, work out (cultivate,
carry out to the goal, and fully complete) your own salvation with
reverence and awe and trembling. (Philippians 2:12, AMP)

Once you settle into a relationship with God, you must deal with
the rest of the mess in your life, and that takes some work.

My decision to trust God completely and to take God's hand followed that same pattern. I made my decision to trust Him at a single
point in time, and He healed my frightened heart on the spot, flooding
me with peace. But I would still have to work out that trust and keep
my eyes on Him every day in practical ways, which was another thing
entirely.

For instance, Mom was still dying. I would have to learn to trust
even in the midst of impending loss and deep sadness. I still had my list
of things that I didn't want to see happen. Could I continue to trust
Him as they continued to happen? There was my nasty habit of "grabbing the future" and worrying intensely about future pain—today. I
knew if I didn't break that habit, I'd never be a woman of trust in my
day-to-day life. Finally, I needed to face the Enemy who had been regularly tormenting me in the night ever since Mom's diagnosis. What
would happen to my trust in the dead of night when everything looked
so dark?

Clearly, my decision to trust the Lord again was only the first step
in restoring my heart. The Lord and I wouldn't be finished until my
mind and habits had been transformed over time. Your decision to fully
trust the Lord again won't fix everything instantly in your heart, any
more than salvation fixes everything on the spot for the new believer.
Fred had to work out his temper problems and work out his purity
issues. And me? I was still overwhelmed by sadness and grief as I began
working out this new life of trust. Your feelings of betrayal and loss will
remain there for you as well, at first.

Still, the restoration of a heart must always start with a decision to trust the Lord fully again. That is why I had to decide to trust Him before I could begin to deal with Mom's terminal illness and, finally, her death. When I made the choice to trust Him, He was freed to release His peace into my heart.

There was still the matter of transforming my mind through hard work and discipline, of course, but by the time a year's worth of sickness and death had passed, I had walked through enough emotionally difficult situations that trusting Him became a habit, just like obedience becomes a habit in the wake of salvation. I had an awareness of His presence during every single thing I went through after that first revelation of peace, even in the things that I had begged Him not to allow. But that peace only came after I made the conscious choice to trust Him for everything that came into my life.

As for your situation, when it comes to your own unintended journey in the wake of your husband's betrayal, you, too, must build up your trust in God before you can rebuild a new life with your husband. From the time you first discover his sexual sin, there's absolutely no more important step you can take than establishing whether you're going to trust the Lord, regardless of the circumstances. Everything in your life is going to hinge upon this question: *Do I trust the Lord, or do I not?*

It's the same for you as it was for me. It's all about control. I couldn't control Mom's cancer, and you can't control this "cancer" of sexual sin. You can't control his wandering eyes or his wandering heart.

Are you still offended with God, kicking against the goads, wrestling to control your husband's actions? Are you clocking your husband on and off the computer, setting up Web nannies and nagging him about missing his accountability group for the last two weeks? Are you traumatized by the prospect of his next mistake and waiting for it to occur? Are you withholding physical intimacy?

Don't misunderstand. We haven't rescinded a word of what we wrote in *Every Heart Restored*, but if you are tightening the screws and scrambling to control your situation before you put your trust fully in the Lord, things will never, ever work out. You must restore your *own* heart before you can help your husband restore his. More important, you must focus more on what God is trying to teach you on this journey than on what God is teaching your husband. God never wastes a crisis, and He doesn't want you to waste this one either. He has a dream of how you'll look on the other end of this ride.

God understands the ripples and aftershocks of an unintended journey. Sure, He'll cry with you because He knows that the fallout is painful, but He also wants to change you so that He can change others around you. Would you really want an instant resurrection of your marital relationship before God has had the chance to fix you too?

A restored heart is always the better choice. A restored heart will place your trauma into His hands so that your hands are free to work out the personal flaws that keep you from living the victorious life. A restored heart rises above the circumstances as you trust that every last thing happening to you will bring about good.

It's funny. Dad's cancer taught me I couldn't trust God with anything. Living through Mom's cancer, I eventually learned that I could trust Him with everything, because He can and will bring the best out of every horrible circumstance. I can honestly look back at my situation and say that while Mom's prognosis and death were the most awful things I could go through and I would never choose to live through them again, I'm now thankful that He allowed these experiences to happen. There may not have been another way to get much-needed changes accomplished in my life.

God is amazing. He can easily manufacture life out of death and joy out of grief. He didn't say, *I need to make some important changes in Brenda, so I'm going to kill off Gwen to get it done.* No, what God did was use Mom's impending death for my good. Everyone dies; He's simply resourceful in using death that way.

It works the same way in your situation. Many men will fall into sexual sin in our sensual culture if they aren't taught how to defend their eyes early. That's inevitable. If your husband has been caught in that snare, you can be sure that God didn't cause your husband to fall into sexual sin in order to make some changes in you. On the other hand, now that it's happened, He's going to be resourceful and use it for your good.

Suffering may be inevitable in this world, but the difference for Christians is that it never need be in vain. Therefore, do not become discouraged in the midst of your trials. Respond to the Lord's pursuit quickly. Trust Him enough to allow Him to use your unintended journey to work in you. Restore your heart together, in intimacy, because there is a legacy at stake.

A Legacy

Have you thought about the legacy you'll leave for others as they watch you learn your way through your messy journey? I was so focused on myself and avoiding pain that I didn't care a whit about what kind of example I was to my children or friends when Mom became very ill. I was aware that others were watching me, but I couldn't even fake a good show.

When I finally made the decision to trust God fully, that action did not go unnoticed by those around me. My daughter Rebecca was especially impacted, as you'll see from her story:

> When Grandma moved into our home shortly after they
> found her cancer, we worshiped and prayed with her every
> night. Grandma would pray out in desperation, "God, please
> heal me of this cancer in my body."

But her longing prayer never ended there. She always found a way to add another sentence, which was, "But, Jesus, Your will be done."

It was easy for me to agree with her because I just "knew" the Lord would heal her. But as it became more and more obvious that Grandma wasn't going to be healed, I became very unhappy with God. *How in the world can God just sit there on His hands? She desperately wants to live, and He obviously doesn't care!*

This didn't seem like the Father I had heard about all my life. He wasn't loving at all. Since He was obviously mean and uncaring, I didn't trust Him anymore with His plans for me. He didn't seem worthy of my praise and respect.

About a month before Grandma died, my mom held me as I cried and cried. "Mom, this all seems to me to be God's fault!" I wailed.

I knew that Mom had been struggling with the same anger and resentment, but I also knew she was doing better. I needed to know what she knew, and that's why I went to her with my feelings. In spite of that, it caught me off guard when Mom asked me, "Do you trust God with whatever happens?"

She wasn't going to trap me. "No," I replied. "He isn't fair, and He doesn't care what happens to me or Grandma!"

I was so angry. My mom talked to me for over two hours, but in the end, it all boiled down to her last words to me as she sent me up to bed. "Just put everything in God's hands, and then you'll have a wonderful peace about the whole situation."

I had given Jesus my heart before, but suddenly I realized that I hadn't surrendered my entire life to Him. I went up to my room by myself and lay down on my bed. I felt completely exhausted from the grief and resentment I had been carrying for so long. Heartbroken and depressed, with tears streaming down my cheeks, I surrendered in desperation, "Lord, I give You everything. It's now in Your hands. I am completely surrendered to You. Whatever You want, let it be done."

The strangest feeling of amazing peace came over me, spreading like a relaxing wave all over my body. I felt a calm contentment sweep through me as a heavy burden of anger and hatred was lifted off me.

Over the next few weeks, even as I watched my grandma decline quickly, I never felt any violent anger at God again. Doubts still lingered though. *Sure, I have peace now, but will it still be there when she dies?*

On Thursday morning, I found out that Grandma had gone into a coma, and I cried until there weren't any tears left. But even in my grief, the peace was still there; yet I still expected the peace to leave the minute she died.

That afternoon, my dad came home, and I knew she was dead before he started his first sentence. I cried harder than I'd ever cried in my life. I knew that no matter how much I wanted Grandma back, I could never touch her or giggle with her or snuggle with her again. In spite of these tormenting thoughts, however, I didn't harbor a trace of anger at God.

Not only was the peace still there, but a fresh belief and trust in Him had been born. I suddenly realized that He had never once left me alone throughout that whole nightmare of Grandma's death. All He wanted to do was hold me in His arms and teach me how to trust Him.

By the time Mom died, I was finally starting to look like the Brenda whom God dreamed of seeing on the other end of the roller-coaster ride, and I was also changing the people around me through His grace.

Rebecca is a part of my legacy, but there are still a couple of things I hope to teach my children and anyone else who cares to listen:

1. *You can restore your heart in God.* If you are not experiencing peace, there is a lack of trust in you. That doesn't mean you are a loser or that God loves you less than everyone else. It means that you have a decision to make, a decision to trust that God can restore a heart in the midst of a harsh, unintended journey like yours.

2. *It takes effort to rebuild your trust in God.* I call this effort the intentional transformation of your mind.

So how do you transform your mind? How do you take every thought captive? How do any of us become imitators of Christ as dearly loved children? These are important questions I want to tackle over the next few chapters so that you can begin to work out the restoration of your heart.

5

Transforming Your Mind

It's important that you understand your responsibility in this transformation. In many churches today, there's a heavy focus on experiencing the Lord. I certainly understand the sentiment, especially when
it comes to an unintended journey. But it is clear from Scripture that
sanctification and transformation have always been a joint effort between the Lord and His children:

> My dear ones, as you have always obeyed [my suggestions],
> so now, not only [with the enthusiasm you would show] in
> my presence but much more because I am absent, work out
> (cultivate, carry out to the goal, and fully complete) your own
> salvation with reverence and awe and trembling (self-distrust,
> with serious caution, tenderness of conscience, watchfulness
> against temptation, timidly shrinking from whatever might
> offend God and discredit the name of Christ).
>
> [Not in your own strength] for it is God Who is all the
> while effectually at work in you [energizing and creating in

you the power and desire], both to will and to work for
His good pleasure and satisfaction and delight. (Philippians
2:12–13, AMP)

If you believe you have no responsibility in the matter, it would also
mean that you are quite happy to wait five, ten, or twenty years until
your husband has an experience with the Lord that finally ends his masturbation habit. Are you willing to kick back and allow your husband's
sexual practices to run their course while you wait for a distaste for porn
and masturbation to meander into his heart? Of course not! He has
responsibilities in this situation, and you know it. And the same is true
for you when it comes to grabbing hold of God. You aren't supposed to
wait. You are to transform your mind intentionally, pursuing it with
everything you've got:

You will seek me and find me when you seek me with all your
heart. (Jeremiah 29:13)

Don't get me wrong here. The Holy Spirit is critical to the process.
The apostle Paul tells us in his New Testament letters that the Holy
Spirit guides, challenges, warns, confirms, renews, and sanctifies. He
even preaches and prays through you, generously distributing ministry
gifts into your hands and pouring God's love all over you. If you want
to experience God more deeply, you'll definitely need to ask your Father
to open up your mind and heart to the Holy Spirit's work.

Having said that, the apostle Paul also suggested that there's a place
for self-discipline in this process. It can be unsettling for some to hear
that the transformation of the mind takes plenty of work and sacrifice,
but I was willing to do anything to grow when I was at my lowest and
feared my emotional life was about to collapse forever. If you are on an
unintended journey, I suspect you're feeling the same kind of urgency.

Over the next four chapters, I will describe what I did to grab hold of God and transform my thinking. My effort had three components:

- Bible study and scripture memorization (chapters 5 and 6)
- prayer, one-on-one worship with God, and fasting (chapter 7)
- two book studies using *Believing God* by Beth Moore and *Tactics* by my husband, Fred Stoeker (chapters 7 and 8)

The words of both authors were very instrumental in my healing, and I'm not just saying that because one of them is my husband. Beth Moore is an awesome and gifted teacher, and I would imagine that her Bible studies are used by millions of women each week. I must have read and studied *Believing God* at least fourteen times since I made the decision to trust God again. She was my safe sister, speaking raw, transforming truth into my heart every single day. Better yet, each reread of the book acted as a check on me to see if I was doing what she had told me to do. *Do I trust God in the way she explains here? Am I actually experiencing intimacy as she discusses it here?* I've never met Beth Moore, but each time I put that book in my hands, I felt like I had a strong, wise, and intimate accountability partner who was fully committed to my growth in God.

As for the second author mentioned, I know him pretty well. But I'm not talking about Fred, my husband; I'm talking about Fred Stoeker, the author.

I think I made it clear in the opening chapter of *The Healing Choice* that Fred—the husband—was a wonderful support as he walked at my side during my journey. From the beginning, I knew I could count on him to be a rock all the way through, and I also knew that he would do whatever he possibly could, without fail. What neither of us knew was that Fred's capabilities as a husband were limited in pushing me back toward God because of my fragile emotional state at the time.

Fred the author was a different story entirely. I had the pleasure of reading *Tactics* before it was published just two months after I'd made my decision to trust God again. It's easily the best of Fred's seven books, but most important, it helped me fall in love with Jesus again.

Tactics was originally targeted toward young single males, but even though you're not among the target audience, I strongly recommend that you pick up a copy. You will gain a greater understanding of the social pitfalls faced by your children as they attempt to stand for purity in this world. Your husband may come to understand His Father's love for him for the first time, helping him to build a vibrant, intimate spiritual life that will transform his battle for purity, just as it has for many middle-aged married men who have read it.

RENEWING

When it comes to restoring your heart and transforming your mind, there's no substitute for studying God's Word. The true wisdom contained in the Word of Christ must take residence in your heart and mind, dwelling within you in all its richness (see Colossians 3:16). Studying God's Word helps you put on the mind of Christ so that you can think like Him and be transformed, reflecting the Lord's glory on your unintended journey (see 2 Corinthians 3:18). Studying God's Word gives you the best opportunity to change the memories—the mental recordings—that bring you down.

Having been raised in as solid a Christian home as you can imagine, I never understood the power of these mental recordings until I married at the age of twenty. Fred had been wounded by years of verbal trauma from the mouth of his father, and these emotional wounds, which became bound up with his temper and his sexuality for years, had also infiltrated his mental recordings and discolored his view of the world. As handsome and dashing as he was to me on the outside, I soon discovered that Fred harbored a darker mind-set that played and re-played the following thoughts within his soul: *I'm no good, and I'm not worthy to stand shoulder to shoulder with the men of this world. No one has ever loved me enough to be completely faithful to me, not even my parents. My marriage will probably end up the same way.*

Changing mental recordings takes time under the best of circumstances, but erasing the lies that play in your mind would be impossible without the written Word. God took Fred's mental patterns and recorded over them with His truth, by His grace.

As our marriage unfolded and Fred got to know me better, he was amazed to see the impact that a solid Christian home can have on a person's life. As far as we knew, I didn't have any false recordings playing in my head. In fact, when he met someone new and was asked to describe me, he'd usually respond, "Brenda's the least neurotic person I've ever met. She's awesome!"

I suppose that's why my emotional collapse in the wake of Mom's diagnosis severely shocked him—and me. Turns out, I had a few false recordings waiting to be played in my head after all, but they'd been gathering dust in the deep recesses of my mind, waiting for the right moment to flip on and trigger a raging fever of incoherent fear.

Those mental recordings told me that since God couldn't be trusted with the big things—like keeping cancer out of Mom's life—it was up to me to deal with her medical situation. When I collapsed, though, I found that I couldn't deal with anything.

When I talk of "transforming the mind" and recording over the mental recordings that drive peace from the heart, I'm talking about breaking the bad mental habits that dim the glory of the Lord in your life and keep you chasing your emotional tail. Studying the Word is central to this work, and it must be the first step you take toward healing your heart.

Sure, some transformation happens just from hanging around church and hearing a sermon once a week. But Jesus had much more in mind for this process:

Christ loved the church and gave himself up for her to make her holy, cleansing her by the washing with water through the word, and to present her to himself as a radiant church, without stain or wrinkle or any other blemish, but holy and blameless. (Ephesians 5:25–27)

Jesus sacrificially, methodically, and intentionally cleanses His church with the Word so that she might be radiant in mind and heart, holy and blameless. This is how cleansing works best, or Jesus wouldn't have chosen to do it in this manner. As part of that church, you need to allow Him to cleanse you in this way.

Intentional transformation is not only possible and desirable but absolutely necessary in the midst of an unintended journey. You need to grow, especially when everything around you lies dead or dying. I chose to grow, and for me that meant making a conscious, committed effort to read and study God's Word so that I could take on God's way of looking at things and rewire the way I thought about Him. Doing so meant choosing to believe that whatever God said was true, no matter what was going on around me and no matter how much I hurt.

I wasn't doing that after we got the cancer diagnosis, though. In fact, discipline and growth were the furthest things from my mind. Instead, I spent all my time begging God to race in and save the day for me. There is certainly a place for that, and I suppose He could have chosen to rush in like the cavalry to save me emotionally, but the Lord had something else in mind. He preferred to teach me the truth, driving my wrongheaded thinking and foolishness far from me so that I could rise above the emotional fray of my circumstances to begin trusting Him. I suspect that's how it will be for you too.

During my journey, the Lord scrubbed my mind with two brands of cleansers:

- the written Word
- the revelatory Word

Let's take a look at how the Lord uses each scrubbing agent and how you might practically and intentionally get the most out of this cleansing process.

The Written Word

Once I made the decision to trust God again after Mom's terminal diagnosis, I desperately needed to hear from Him regularly. After all, communication is the essence of a relationship, and Fred encouraged me to remember that studying the Word was the same as having a personal experience with God. Something Fred wrote in his book *Tactics* had a huge impact following my collapse, and this passage was especially crucial for me:

> Maybe Bible reading isn't exactly the kind of experience you have in mind when you dream of experiencing God.
>
> If so, you've forgotten that the Bible is the Word of God. The Bible is a living document and extremely active in shaping the thoughts and attitudes of your heart (see Hebrews 4:12). Recall, too, that Jesus is the Living Word of God, in the flesh (see John 1:14). Therefore, an encounter with the Bible is an encounter with Jesus.
>
> This point is so critical to understand. You will always be as close to God as you want to be, and the simplest way to get close to Him is through His written Word. Every time you crack open a Bible, you are getting into His presence. If you want to be close to the Lord, you must seek these Scripture encounters with Him with all of your heart. (*Tactics,* 187–88)

Do you want to get close to Jesus and hear from Him? Then open your Bible. He's there for you, right now, and He's anxious to have you sit a little closer. I'd like to take a moment to share how I approached this.

First of all, once I was convinced that reading God's Word would bring me closer to Him, I made this spiritual discipline the most important priority in my life. I had to let other things go by the wayside for the greater goal of transforming my heart and my mind. Mom was dying, and the pain and torment of my collapse was in my face every moment of every day, so I had neither the time nor the luxury to dawdle. I had to either transform my mind or lose my sanity, so I felt pressed to go after transformation with everything I had.

What fell by the wayside? It could be anything, depending upon the day. Sometimes I wouldn't get my house cleaned completely. On another day, I might not get the laundry done. Perhaps I wouldn't sit and read a novel or watch some DVD because my new spiritual discipline of studying the Bible trumped entertaining myself. I viewed the Word as literal food for my soul. I had to be fed to be transformed.

This may sound funny, but in light of my desperation, I actually had to cut down on my Bible reading. Let me explain. Before Mom got sick, I was in the habit of reading through the entire Bible once a year, which you can usually do by reading about three chapters a day. To be honest, I'd often breeze through the half-dozen pages to meet my daily quota, and then I'd forget what I'd just read within ten minutes.

During my trials with Mom's sickness, though, I couldn't remember what I read after ten seconds! I knew I had to make some adjustments because my mind was scattered. I couldn't expect to peruse three chapters and have my reading impact me. So I decided instead to read only one or two chapters and really focus on those couple of pages. Then I would read them a couple more times, pondering two questions:

1. *What is the Lord saying to me today?*
2. *What can I learn from this today?*

Even if what I read in the Bible didn't seem to apply to Mom's situation, asking those questions focused my attention on the Holy Spirit and what He wanted to impress upon me.

Cutting back on how much I read of the Bible helped, but there were still too many times when the stress would sweep away my comprehension of my daily Bible reading within the hour. While I knew that God's Word stayed in my spirit all day long no matter what I did, since the Word of God is living and active and penetrates even to dividing soul and spirit (see Hebrews 4:12), the problem was that what I read wasn't staying in my mind. That's where I desperately needed it.

So I came up with a simple solution. I picked up some three-by-five note cards with the same strip of adhesive found on the back of Post-its. I took one note card each morning, put the date and the scripture reference in the upper-right corner, and then as I studied the Word that morning, I wrote several highlights or key points on the card. Then I took that note card with me wherever I went that day. I put it at the top of my computer monitor when I checked my e-mail. I put it on the kitchen windowsill when I did dishes. I put it on the steering wheel of the car and read it when I drove around doing errands. (Just kidding! But I read it at stoplights.) After dinner, I put it nearby whenever I ironed clothes. All day long, I was reminded of what I learned from the Word that day.

Let me give you an example of what I might write on a note card. Mom died in June 2006, but one April morning before that, I happened to be reading Philippians 1 and 2 and wrote the following:

- Paul's perseverance in a difficult situation (prison) gave other Christians the ability "to speak the word of God more courageously and fearlessly" (1:14). If we do well in our circumstances (for example, Mom's sickness), maybe we can also encourage others to do better.
- It doesn't matter what the motive is as long as Christ is preached. Paul rejoiced.
- Conduct yourself in a manner worthy of the gospel of Christ. God is at work in us both "to will and to act according to his good purpose" (2:13).

At first glance, I thought only the first point had anything to do with Mom's sickness, but rereading my notes through the day helped me see how the second and third points related to my situation too. Whatever happened to Mom, it was important that Christ be preached and that I conduct myself in a manner worthy of the gospel of Christ. God was at work in me to do His will.

Let's take a look at another note card from that same month, this one from 1 Timothy 4–5:

- We should work hard at godly disciplines—be absorbed in them—so that we will have progress evident to all.
- If any widow has children or grandchildren, they must first learn godliness by taking care of her needs. This is the most basic thing that we should learn to be faithful at.
- We are constantly nourished by words of the faith. How important it is to not neglect Bible reading and scripture memory.
- Aim for godliness with contentment.

Throughout the day I would remind myself of these timeless truths so that both my heart and mind could be restored. As the daughter of a widow, I asked myself if we were meeting Mom's physical and emotional needs, and I could honestly say yes. That encouraged me. Then I remembered how Mom had helped me memorize dozens of Scripture verses as a young girl—verses that I could call upon in times of stress, which encouraged me even further.

Reciting Scripture from memory prompted me to think about memorizing new verses that seemed pertinent to what I was going through. Over the next couple of months, I thumbed through Scripture and gathered verses that applied to the trials in my life and fundamental truths that I wanted to plant deep within my heart. I put these verses into four groups and wrote them on four sticky note cards, which meant I would review them every four days, one each day. I stuck each day's note card next to my Bible-highlights note card wherever I went, constantly poring over it and watching for how it applied to me in each situation.

I also hunted up a group of verses on suffering and reviewed them every single day, using regular-sized, colored Post-its for these. Occasionally I would run across another verse in my Bible reading that would jump out at me, and I would add that into the mix as well. I called these *trial verses,* because they helped me retrain my mind to trust God in the midst of the trials.

Here is my list of trial verses, and I recommend that you write them down or print them from the Internet (BibleGateway.com has a great search engine for Scripture verses) for review and refreshment throughout the day. I've included a few verses here in their entirety to give you a flavor for them now as you're reading, but I've only listed the references for others in the interest of space:

> I am always with you;
> you hold me by my right hand.
> You guide me with your counsel,
> and afterward you will take me into glory.
> Whom have I in heaven but you?
> And earth has nothing I desire besides you.
> My flesh and my heart may fail,
> but God is the strength of my heart
> and my portion forever. (Psalm 73:23–26)

> Consider it pure joy, my brothers, whenever you face trials of many kinds, because you know that the testing of your faith develops perseverance. Perseverance must finish its work so that you may be mature and complete, not lacking anything. (James 1:2–4)

We are hard pressed on every side, but not crushed; perplexed,
but not in despair; persecuted, but not abandoned; struck down,
but not destroyed. (2 Corinthians 4:8–9)

I also suggest Psalms 18:1–3; 46:1–2; Isaiah 40:28–31; Matthew
6:34; 2 Corinthians 4:16–18; 10:3–5; 12:9; and Hebrews 12:7–11.

Next on my list were *filter verses,* which I needed to keep my filters
clear during my unintended journey. I'd become furious at God, as if
He had been mistreating me, but He hadn't been mistreating me at all,
as Scripture reminded me. Suffering is just part of life. Changing those
mental recordings, though, required more than a head decision. Emotional content and context had to be involved, and that is where the
Word comes into the picture.

Understanding the true source of your trials and tribulations will
keep you from misinterpreting God's character through your circumstances, so it is also important to review these scriptures every day as well.

First Fundamental Truth
God is good at all times. He'll never change.

Because of the LORD's great love we are not consumed,
for his compassions never fail.
They are new every morning;
great is your faithfulness.
I say to myself, "The LORD is my portion;
therefore I will wait for him." (Lamentations 3:22–24)

Every good gift and every perfect gift is from above, and comes
down from the Father of lights, with whom there is no variation
or shadow of turning. (James 1:17, NKJV)

I also suggest Psalm 25:7–9 and Matthew 7:11.

Second Fundamental Truth

God is my precious Father, and I'm the apple of His eye. He will complete what He has authored in me, and He'll never love anyone more than He loves me.

> I will be a Father to you, and you will be my sons and daughters, says the Lord Almighty. (2 Corinthians 6:18)

> I thank my God upon every remembrance of you, always
> in every prayer of mine making request for you all with joy,
> for your fellowship in the gospel from the first day until now,
> being confident of this very thing, that He who has begun a
> good work in you will complete it until the day of Jesus Christ.
> (Philippians 1:3–6, NKJV)

> I also suggest Deuteronomy 32:9–11 and Psalm 63:2–3.

Third Fundamental Truth

Christ overcame the world, but I'll still have trials and tribulations because a third-party intruder (Satan) retains temporary dominion on earth.

> These things I have spoken to you, that in Me you may have
> peace. In the world you will have tribulation; but be of good
> cheer, I have overcome the world. (John 16:33, NKJV)

> It was good for me to be afflicted
>   so that I might learn your decrees.
> The law from your mouth is more precious to me
>   than thousands of pieces of silver and gold.
>   (Psalm 119:71–72)

> I also suggest Psalm 91:4–6 and Romans 8:16–18.

From Fred

Brenda's new discipline of writing down key takeaway points on note cards and hanging them around the house had a profound effect on me. Perhaps I can best explain what I mean in the context of this Scripture passage:

> Wives, in the same way be submissive to your husbands so that, if any of them do not believe the word, they may be won over without words by the behavior of their wives, when they see the purity and reverence of your lives. Your beauty should not come from outward adornment, such as braided hair and the wearing of gold jewelry and fine clothes. Instead, it should be that of your inner self, the unfading beauty of a gentle and quiet spirit, which is of great worth in God's sight. For this is the way the holy women of the past who put their hope in God used to make themselves beautiful. (1 Peter 3:1–5)

To be honest, I never cared much for the first part of this passage. First of all, how does a wife's silence influence a husband anyway? The passage irritated me and never made much sense, especially when I heard testimonies like one I heard in church about a woman whose husband was overbearing, withering, and unsaved.

It seems that the woman had a Christian neighbor who also lived with an unsaved spouse. One day after talking, they made a covenant to quietly pray together for their husbands' salvation. When believers are married to unbelievers, God instructs them to pray precisely in this way while living godly lives. Their obedience was rewarded thirteen years later when their husbands accepted Christ on the very same day! Tears streamed from my eyes as I listened to their story from my pew.

But later, I sat back and did the math. Jasen was five years old at the time, and I thought, *Man, if I refuse to change and make Brenda suffer through thirteen long years of prayer over me, Jasen will be eighteen and leaving home. It will be too late for him.*

That's why I don't like 1 Peter 3:1–2. While Peter directed his message to wives with non-Christian husbands, many Christian men overlook an inconvenient truth and use those verses to muzzle their wives and thereby inflict collateral damage on their children. *If you don't like something in me,* they bark, *keep it to yourself, woman! Just shut up and pray for me.*

Frankly, that's sick, and it gives me nightmares to think where we'd be today if Brenda had kept her thoughts to herself regarding my behavior over the years. But just as my daughter-in-law Rose showed me that silence can be a form of pursuit, Brenda showed me how silent behavior can influence a man profoundly.

When Brenda started doing her note-card thing, she didn't tell me what she was doing, but it wasn't long before I started seeing these sticky notes everywhere I turned. I'd get in the car and see a sticky note stuck to the steering wheel. I'd go to get a bowl of cereal and see one pasted to the cupboard. I'd go into the master bath to clean up for bed and see one stuck on the mirror. It seemed positively loony.

I let things go for a couple of weeks, but finally my curiosity bubbled over. "What's up with all these sticky notes all over the place, sweetheart?"

"You know how I've always told you that when I read my Bible in the morning, it all just flies straight out of my head?" she queried. I nodded. "Well, I just can't afford that anymore. Times are too desperate for me. I have to know the Lord better. I can't just talk to Him once a day anymore. I can't afford to have these truths missing from my mind for twenty-three out of every twenty-four hours."

I simply cannot explain what that did in my heart. This was my Brenda, the one who runs to the couch with a historical novel at the mere sniff of stress, and the one who had collapsed spiritually in utter failure just a few weeks earlier. Yet there she was, fighting her way out of the pit like a fierce badger, but doing it quietly, with a deep, burning resolve.

As I watched her quiet determination over the next few months, Brenda became more intensely beautiful to me than I'd ever remembered. The last time something caught me off guard like this was when I made a covenant with my eyes to stop looking at the sensual women around me. Once Brenda became the only woman I was looking at and my sexuality was aimed only at her, she began to look stunningly gorgeous to me, like a supermodel. I couldn't keep my eyes or my hands off her.

But the nature of this attraction was very different. I couldn't even understand what kind of beauty I was sensing. It wasn't sensual or sexual, but it was an overwhelming draw; a calm, deep passion of the heart; a respect and an honor bubbling up from my deepest core that was extremely compelling.

About that time I ran across the apostle Peter's words again, and I had my answer. I knew instantly that this must be the unfading beauty of a quiet and gentle spirit that Peter was writing about. "For this is the way the holy women of the past who put their hope in God used to make themselves beautiful," he wrote in 1 Peter 3:5.

Good choice, I thought. I don't know what you are currently doing to look beautiful, my friend, but whatever it is, this is way better. The spiritual disciplines will not only transform your mind and restore the heart within you, but they just might restore a deep passion between the two of you in your marriage.

A Revelatory Word

So what am I (Brenda) talking about when I speak of a revelatory word? Let me give you an example. My mother died on June 15, and I wrote this on the morning of July 13, less than a month after her death:

I had a revelation from God last night, so I've been up since 3:30 a.m. I suddenly realized that while I've given Mom up physically, I hadn't yet given her up emotionally. I realized I needed to give it all to the Lord if I were to truly take His hand and look to the future.

The Lord revealed to me that though my relationship with Mom was wonderful, this relationship was like the other earthly things that we grasp too tightly and that keep us from moving ahead with the Lord.

As I wrestled with this thought, I discovered what the Lord wanted to do for me. He knew my guilt was still heavy. I had been the one who touched every base for Mom for twenty-five years to make sure she was taken care of, but during her sickness, I missed quite a few bases. When she was first diagnosed, I fell apart and couldn't keep her in my home like she wanted me to. I couldn't talk to her because my weakness prevented approaching parts of our relationship. When she was in a coma, I couldn't help her. I was so afraid she had been disappointed in me, that I'd let her down in her deepest hour of need.

As I thought on this, God revealed that only He can cover every base, and since I couldn't, I shouldn't feel guilty about it. I could only do what I could do back then, and the rest was His job to handle. My guilt was also His job to handle, and He wanted to handle it right now for me.

So I began to name the awful memories that had been bothering me and give them over to the Lord to keep, one by one. Like the tortured, endless hours of her coughing, and how it would get so bad that she could barely gasp, "Beat me." Then I'd thump her back until her throat was clear.

Then there was the time a few days before she died when her mind was going and she thought she was back at home. I saw the hurt on her face when she knew she wasn't making sense, but she was unable to sort out her confused state or do anything about it. I found that if I broke things down and handed the painful things to the Lord one by one, I could be rid of them. I wouldn't pick them back up to obsess over them again.

When I finished giving these awful memories to the Lord, I smiled. I began to think about how rich I was in having had Mom as my mother, and it occurred to me that every one of my assets on earth was only borrowed, including my richest human assets. I realized that while she was a huge part of my life and I would keep many of her good things in my character and memory, my relationship with Mom had only been mine for a season. What had been earthly had been moved to the heavenly realm. Since I was still on earth, I needed to turn my attention to what God had for my future and where He was leading me here.

The Lord then reminded me of something Corrie ten Boom taught me in one of her books: hold on loosely to the things of this world. We don't normally think of dear family members as things of this world that are temporary and come and go, but the Lord was showing me that our relationships are as earthly as a favorite old bicycle that you've finally outgrown or a gorgeous

*apartment in San Francisco that you'll never see
again. Only the Lord is permanent.*

*So I began thanking Him for all the good things
Mom and I had together. The many, many wonderful
years of enduring friendship. The phone calls and the
laughter. The countless trips and warm holidays. I
thanked God for each of them, and then asked Him
to keep them for me.*

*It was a huge emotional step for me last night—
examining the things in my life with Mom and giving
them to God for safekeeping, and then choosing to let
go of her hand and, in trust, taking God's hand for the
future.*

From Fred

Revelatory words are incredibly transforming. When Brenda woke up
and started telling me what she'd experienced the night before, I immediately heard the change in her. Suddenly, a light had clicked on, and
she was speaking with authority and excitement. After she'd shared her
story about the revelation with me, she immediately headed to her desk
and began laying out all the details for sorting through her mom's
earthly possessions, something she'd had no energy to even discuss until
that moment.

Just a single phrase from the Lord can turn your mind around per-
manently. But you have to seek it. Recently my daughter Laura, my precious "Peanut," was preparing to leave for North Carolina to attend
graduate school, and she was terrified, knowing she was moving halfway
across the country for the next seven years to pursue a dual graduate
degree—a doctorate in veterinary medicine and a PhD in microbiology.
During that summer I gave her a crash course in my book *Tactics,* hoping she'd glimpse her heavenly Father for who He is—her loving Father,

not just her glorious King. I told her that she needed a revelation of His heart or she'd be hard pressed to find the peace she needed to move east. After a month or two, she said she had never had a revelation in her life and asked me to explain exactly what it was she should be looking for.

So I began to share the story of the most transforming moment I've ever experienced with the Lord, which took place during a Christian seminar for guys one July evening in Colorado as I listened to Greg Laurie open things up on Friday evening with a salvation message. While I'd been saved years before, I was still struggling with deep issues regarding my relationship with my dominating father, and these old wounds were severely affecting my relationship with Brenda and my kids through my angry temper. I needed some answers badly.

In the middle of his talk, Greg mentioned that our achievements do not impress God, because He is behind them all anyway. "God doesn't arch His eyebrows and give a low whistle when He sees that I'm the pastor of a church with ten thousand members," Greg said. "It doesn't impress Him that I'm on stage right now talking to fifty thousand men. He doesn't really need that from me—He could use anyone. In fact, when it comes to our relationship together, it doesn't matter to Him whether I'm successful or not. The same goes for each of you out there."

Then Greg paused for a moment before making a simple statement that blew me away. "The truth is, all God wants is to put His arm around you and have a steak with you." Instantly, God's revelation crashed through my spirit like a shooting star.

After retelling that story to my daughter, I said solemnly, "Laura, I know Greg's word picture sounds pretty simple, yet when his words were mixed with God's power in my spirit, all those years of pain and frustration over my dad crumbled into dust, just like that. Suddenly, I could see everything. Unlike my father down here, my heavenly Father already saw me as His son. I didn't have to prove myself to anyone. After that moment, I never struggled with any of those issues again."

Laura had been listening carefully to my story because she wanted to understand what it was that I was hoping God would do for her. Suddenly, she burst out laughing. "That's it?" she snorted. "That phrase about the steak did all that? I don't get it at all."

I began laughing with her. "I know it sounds crazy, but the Holy Spirit knew exactly what I needed to hear. He's a master because He knows you through and through! He will take a scripture, a phrase from a pastor's message, anything at all, but He'll find something that will click only with you. Then He'll flood it with power and break down the walls in your life, just like that."

"Well, when will that happen for me?" she asked.

"Who knows?" I shrugged. "Tomorrow. Next week. Next month."

We sat silently for a moment. I could still see her grinning over my story, but I was struggling inside. Three nights in a row we'd been talking about the things of the Lord as we read portions of *Tactics* together, and the Lord had prompted me to pray with her each night, but each time, I passed; for some reason, it felt funny to do it. This time I had no choice.

"Laura, let's pray about this."

So I laid my hands on her head and prayed, *Lord, please show my daughter what it means to hear a revelatory Word from You. As her father, I ask that You give her a phrase, a verse, any old thing. Just turn on the lights for her. I've been trying to show her how passionately You feel toward her, but I haven't quite gotten through the way I've longed to. Lord, please do it for us.*

About a week later, I had another moment with Laura that added to my long list of special times with my kids. As she talked again about her fear of leaving home and heading east for what seemed like the rest of her life, I began talking to her about the heart an earthly father has for his children and how he dedicates his life to grooming their gifts. In doing so, I was hoping she would finally catch a glimpse of how her heavenly Father's heart beats for her.

"You know, Laura, I had always wanted Jasen to get interested in sports, and I was looking forward to tossing the ball around and sending him to football camp and doing everything I could to make him a star," I began. "But he didn't like football. He liked computers, which I knew nothing about. Still, since I loved him, I went ahead and sent him to computer camp, and though I've never been able to share his passion for computers, it was still exciting to see him grow into everything he'd hoped to be.

"Laura, you have a gift for scientific research, and I can't share that with you any more than I can share computer science with Jasen. I can't go to North Carolina and live with you there. But the Lord, your Father, is going with you to the East Coast, and He will get to share every last detail of this journey with you."

Laura wants to be head of the Food and Drug Administration one day. So, lightly playing off the joyous-dad-sending-his-son-to-football-camp imagery I'd used when talking about Jasen and me, I said, "Your heavenly Father is excited out of His mind about your future because He knows what you're made of, and He's sitting on His throne leaning over to Jesus, saying, 'Me and Peanut are heading off to FDA camp at North Carolina State together, and we're going to have fun!' "

There it was. I didn't know it at the time, but three nights later, she came to me and began to cry.

"What's wrong, Peanut?" I asked, stroking her hair.

"Daddy, I just wanted you to know that I had my revelation a few nights ago. You remember when you said the phrase 'Me and Peanut are heading off to FDA camp together'?"

I nodded. Who could forget such a silly little phrase, especially my calling a rigorous seven-year graduate-school program "FDA camp"?

"Well, that was the moment, Daddy. I don't know how God did it. It was you talking, but somehow He was talking to me through your words too. Anyway, until that moment when the Lord used my nickname and called me Peanut, I never realized how much He treasures me and sees me as His own precious little girl. Daddy, I know what you mean now when you say that a revelation can change everything. Once I heard Him use my nickname, my relationship with Him will never be the same. I feel safe to move to North Carolina now, and I know everything will be okay."

Amazing.

You can experience something like this with the Lord as well, and it all starts with prayer. Ask the Lord to reveal His love to you in a personal, touching way like He did with Laura. Ask Him to make all the difference in your life through His written Word and through the Spirit's gentle touch.

You're the apple of His eye, and He longs for you to draw closer to Him. Trust Him. Whether you're trying to let go emotionally or searching for a way to face the future without fear, move in closer to Him. He's waiting for you to snuggle up so He can whisper in your ear exactly what you need to hear.

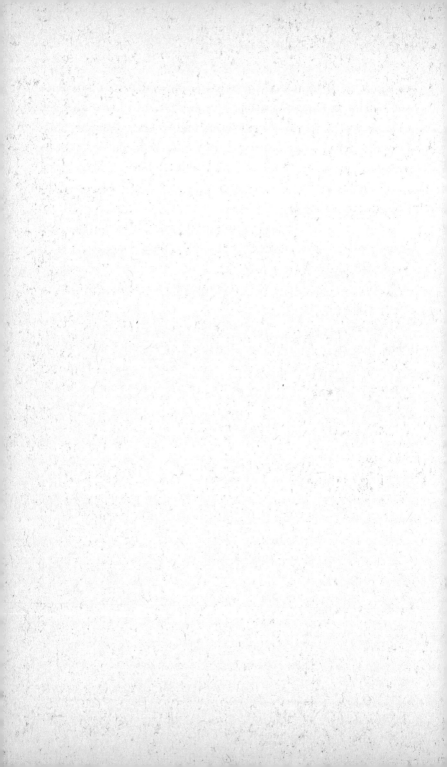

6

The Anchor

FROM BRENDA

After Mom received the news that her mesothelioma was untreatable and she had only six months to live, I packed her into the car and headed home to Des Moines to care for her. When we arrived, Fred herded us into the family room to discuss our feelings and how we might approach this crisis together as a family.

Without telling anyone his plans, he began leaving work early. At four o'clock Fred would head to Blue Chapel at our church to pray and worship for an hour. He'd attack the Enemy with the Word—the sword of the Spirit—with all of his heart. For a full month, he fasted every other day, abstaining from food completely on those days. When we heard what he was doing, Mom was moved to tears by his love for her. She whispered, "Freddie, you have gone way beyond the call of duty. I never expected this." That was a pair of the most indelible sentences ever spoken to Fred, words he'll treasure to his *own* grave.

But that wasn't the only treasure that was unearthed during those awesome days. Somewhere in the middle of that conflagration, the Lord told Fred to instruct me to read and study Psalm 139 every single day to help heal my heart. As you recall, I wasn't listening to the Lord's voice in those days, so He needed to get His message through to me by other means.

Trouble is, I wasn't listening all that much to Fred those days either. When he mentioned what the Lord had suggested to me, I shrugged my shoulders and read the whole chapter the first night but then didn't read it again for a couple of weeks. I hadn't yet bought into this plan. Then one afternoon as Fred battled again in Blue Chapel, the Lord pulled him aside during a lull in the action and mentioned that He hadn't seen me reading Psalm 139 in a while.

When he got home, Fred made an excuse for us to get away from the house. As we drove around the neighborhood, he casually asked, "So how has Psalm 139 been working out for you?"

Looking out the window, I mumbled, "Not that well… I haven't been reading it." No use lying about it; I was never very good at hiding my thoughts from Fred anyway.

"Brenda, I'm glad you admitted it, because I already knew you haven't been!" he said firmly. He paused for a moment, and I felt his frustration rising. "How fair is it for you to ignore what God is offering to you as help when you're collapsing and putting pressure on everyone in our house? We're all with you, sweetheart, and I love you with everything I am. I know you can't help this collapse, but you can help whether or not you read a simple psalm once a day. I need you to listen, sweetheart. I expect you to do what's right, and all of us need you to do what's right. Will you please start reading Psalm 139 for me every day?"

What could I say? Chastened, and with eyes pooling, I replied, "I'm so sorry, and I know you're right. Yes, I will start reading it."

I did—twice a day—and am I ever glad. Psalm 139 became my "anchor chapter," the section of Scripture that buoyed my sinking ship.

Each time I opened my Bible, I would pick that psalm apart verse by verse, thought by thought, and apply God's words to what I was going through that day. I discovered an incredible wealth of encouragement and truth in Psalm 139, and as someone stuck on an unintended journey, I was amazed how a single chapter could do so much to heal my heart. I thoroughly recommend that you read and study Psalm 139 twice a day, morning and evening, as you wrestle with your husband's sexual sin.

Studying God's Word over and over is worthwhile—even vital—and that goes double when you're traveling on an unintended journey. Out in these churning seas, the losses come in endless waves, and you need that daily reminder of God's truth so that you're not swamped, forgetting everything you know.

God's Word is like a mooring that holds you in place, and that's something you need because tidal grief wants to sweep you away in its relentless, pounding surf. For me, Mom's terminal illness was awful because it flipped my entire life upside down, but I'd say the worst part was having no idea how long it would last. Even though her doctors were talking about a matter of months, I felt like I would never step out from under that dark cloud. I had no faith that life would ever be happy and normal again.

Once Mom moved back to Moline, we visited her each weekend and, later on, twice a week. With each trip, we'd detect more deterioration in her health, such as less energy or the use of more oxygen. The days and weeks dragged on. How long would I be trapped in this surreal existence where nothing of any note happened in my life—except for more grief?

This surreal existence took over every aspect of our lives. We didn't socialize with friends because we were too busy preparing for our next trip to Moline or catching up from the last one. For the Stoeker family, there would be no vacations or weekend getaways while Mom was still alive. Basically, we were handling the details of running two full house-holds simultaneously, half a state apart.

Our routine was to depart from home Friday night so we could awake early on Saturday at Mom's house to clean it and to prepare meals for her to eat during the coming week. In the afternoon we'd hit Rudy's for tacos, pick up our favorite shakes at Whitey's, and then return to Mom's to mow grass and keep up the yard. On Sunday mornings, we'd go to church, try to enjoy lunch at T.G.I. Friday's, and then go back to Mom's house to finish up with more jobs, errands, and cooking before packing up for the two-and-a-half-hour drive that would get us back to Des Moines around eight o'clock. The considerable gas and restaurant bills were adding up, yet every Monday morning I'd wake up to begin planning the following week's cycle.

As exhausting as life was at that time, and as awful as Mom's life had become, I knew that once she died, everything would be even worse! In my mind, the level of grief and pain of loss would only intensify once I lost her.

Turns out I was right. After she was gone, "layers of loss" began to unfold. These were the things that I longed to share with Mom, but she wasn't there. She loved a fun graduation party, and we had three of them—for Jasen, Laura, and Rebecca—the first year she was gone, but she wasn't there. She wasn't around when Jasen walked down the aisle following his marriage to Rose. She didn't bake us a cake from scratch when Fred and I celebrated our twenty-fifth wedding anniversary. While she practically lived for Boston terriers, she wasn't there with us to pick up Laura's newest canine friend, Lucy Lou. She wasn't on the phone with us popping every button the day Laura accepted her full-ride, dual-degree research scholarship at North Carolina State.

And when I became a mother-in-law, I didn't have a clue how to handle my new role. Mom, the perfect mother-in-law, would have been great to talk to, but I couldn't phone her. After two of my children moved away for the first time, one to Minnesota and another to North Carolina, she wasn't there to ask, *What was it like for you when I left, Mom? What do I do with these pieces of my heart?* But you know what? While I once thought only Mom could fulfill that role of intimate confidante, Psalm 139 reminded me again and again that Jesus was ready to take on that role. He had asked for my hand earlier, and I had taken His. Now I had to learn to be comfortable there at His side.

He wanted me to talk to Him about everything in my life now. He wanted me to get closer and closer until He was the one I would emotionally depend upon. I found that rereading Psalm 139 and studying those words was the same as studying Him, and I grew to love what I saw in Him.

You need to take His hand and get comfortable at His side as well, especially if you're struggling over your husband's sexual sin. I'm sure you're dealing with that same feeling of endlessness, a feeling that you'll never find your way out of the rain. It's especially true for you if your husband wasn't honorable up front, meaning that he did his best to hide this sin from you. If you discovered his secret sin accidentally, you're left wondering whether he is really repentant or just real sorry he got caught. Trust takes a long, long time to be restored with these doubts in your mind.

Many women—blindsided and appalled at the same time—wonder what hit them. They thought they had the perfect marriage, but now they look ahead soberly and see only grief. *Will my life ever be happy again? Will I ever trust him again?*

Sure, it's now all out in the open, and he's pledged to stop, but intuitively you know that whole new layers of grief and loss could appear during the ebb and flow of your husband's battle, like when he swears on a stack of Bibles that he's clean and then you catch him masturbating to a *Playboy* centerfold some night. That'll shatter your heart into a thousand pieces.

When stuff like that happens, it's tough to grab hold of God and keep Him close, especially if you aren't used to depending upon Him like I was. You need a picture of your King that makes you smile again, one that calls His beautiful image into your mind again and again. You need thoughts that restore your heart and transform your mind, and that comes from reading Scripture.

The Lord may give you a different chapter of Scripture to be your anchor. Since He knows you through and through, He knows exactly what you need, but if you need a good place to start, I recommend that you adopt Psalm 139. As your sister in Christ and a charter member of your support group, I'd like to relate what I was thinking when I picked this chapter apart daily to find His heart.

> O LORD, you have searched me
>   and you know me.
> You know when I sit and when I rise;
>   you perceive my thoughts from afar.
> You discern my going out and my lying down;
>   you are familiar with all my ways.
> Before a word is on my tongue
>   you know it completely, O LORD. (verses 1–4)

In these first four verses, the Lord says that He searches you, knows you, and is familiar with all your ways. The word *familiar* doesn't just mean He sort of knows you. He really knows every little thing about who you are, all you do, and even the way you react to little things, which reminds me of a simple story that Fred told about me in *Every Man's Battle*.

Fred loves to wander through bookstores, and one time while we were running errands, he asked if he could run into our favorite bookstore and pick up a book he had been intending to read. I said fine and waited in the car while he hustled inside.

Fred grabbed his book and approached the cashier. She asked if he was a member of their frequent customer program, and Fred replied in the affirmative. He thought nothing of it until the cashier announced that his past purchases had earned him a five-dollar gift certificate. The cashier asked whether she should apply it to his current purchase. A smile came across his face. "No, I'll save it for my wife," he replied. "She'll be real excited about it."

Just about then I was wondering, *What's taking him so long?* After hopping out of the car, I found him kibitzing with the cashier. "Watch this," I heard him say.

"Look what I've got," he said with a huge grin, waving a piece of paper with his right hand.

I grabbed the coupon from him and squealed with delight. "Ooh, this is great—five dollars!" I exclaimed.

Winking at the cashier, Fred grinned again. "What did I tell you?"

She laughed along with him. I adore being Fred's beloved, and I cherish how he's studied me and now knows me through and through. But I am also my Lord's beloved. While He patiently let me hold my Mom's hand for oh-so-many years, He loved me so much that He could hardly wait any longer. He had to have my hand and my whole heart.

Although these initial verses talk about the outward things—like knowing when you sit and when you rise—they also refer to your inner thoughts. He knows the words on your tongue before you speak them; still He listens intently to what you have to say. He thinks you're precious and can't wait to get His presence embedded in your life even more deeply.

When I was going through my traumatic year with Mom, I sometimes felt so lonely that I didn't think anybody could understand what I was going through. After I read Psalm 139 consistently for a couple of weeks, Jesus came to me through these verses and reassured me that He knew every little thing about me, so I wasn't really alone. The lonely feelings were just feelings.

If you have recently discovered your husband's sexual sin, you will feel intensely lonely at times. I greatly encourage you to return daily to Psalm 139 and be reminded that you are not alone and that your Beloved loves you through and through.

You hem me in—behind and before;
    you have laid your hand upon me.
Such knowledge is too wonderful for me,
    too lofty for me to attain. (verses 5–6)

When I first read this passage, it bothered me for days. At the time, I was running from anything that had to do with Mom's sickness. In my self-focus, these verses seemed to be saying, *You hemmed me in, You laid Your hand upon me, and now You've trapped me with this cancer!*

I felt like He had me strapped down tight on a gurney. But as I continued to meditate on these verses in context, I understood that He didn't mean He'd trapped me into some foul circumstance He'd orchestrated. Instead He was saying that He is with me during every unintended journey, protecting me on all sides with His presence and placing His hand over me as a cover.

You are literally covered on all sides. In other words, He's got your back, and because you're His beloved, He never takes His eyes off you.

Where can I go from your Spirit?
    Where can I flee from your presence?
If I go up to the heavens, you are there;
    if I make my bed in the depths, you are there.
If I rise on the wings of the dawn,
    if I settle on the far side of the sea,
even there your hand will guide me,
    your right hand will hold me fast. (verses 7–10)

The Anchor   113

It meant so much to know that there wasn't a place where He wasn't with me. When I was sitting in Mom's backyard on the scariest day of my life, waiting for my brothers, Brent and Barry, to bring Mom back from the doctor with the final diagnosis, God was with me. If I did something from my list of things that I'd prayed desperately not to have to do, like drive to the Quad Cities alone and take Mom away from her beloved house for the very last time, I had His promise. If I sat in dread at the hospice, spending all day alone with her when everything inside me was screaming to run, He was with me.

But what if it's midnight and your husband's away on a three-day business trip and you're lying in wide-eyed dread in bed, desperately hoping he'll stay clean? Guess what? God is there. Through every one of the hard things you face, the strength of His Word enables you to look in the mirror and say to yourself, *He is here with me, and there is nowhere that I can go that He is not with me.*

Psalm 139 was especially critical during the early days of Mom's sickness when my commitment to Him was on the verge of crumbling. I cried out, *Lord, don't let me fall away from You!*

He was right there, assuring me that His hand would guide me and hold me fast. He wasn't about to let me fall, no matter what my circumstances were or how much I hurt.

> If I say, "Surely the darkness will hide me
>   and the light become night around me,"
> even the darkness will not be dark to you;
>   the night will shine like the day,
>   for darkness is as light to you. (verses 11–12)

During Mom's final year, a cloud of darkness hung over me, a terrible darkness that wouldn't disperse. Yet once I learned these verses and believed that His Word was true for me, I recognized that I could not possibly be standing in the darkness alone because His Spirit and presence were always with me, and wherever He is, the darkness is light. Nowhere are things so dark that His presence does not light it up.

If your husband's sexual sin has covered your heart in a darkness that you can practically feel, run to Him and snuggle in—and watch the darkness turn to light.

> For you created my inmost being;
> > you knit me together in my mother's womb.
> I praise you because I am fearfully and wonderfully made;
> > your works are wonderful,
> > I know that full well. (verses 13–14)

These iconic verses from the Bible contain so much depth and so much meaning. When Mom was about to be torn from me for the rest of my time on earth, all I could think about was the total separation. She'd be gone. But when I read, "You knit me together in my mother's womb," and then meditated on this verse day after day, a light came on in my mind. I realized that there could never be total separation from Mom because I was created there, in her womb. She's a part of me, and she will always be a part of me, which gave me enormous comfort.

Perhaps this truth won't apply directly to your journey with your husband's sexual sin, but it does point out again that Scripture is a living Word and that God can use it to speak to us no matter how unique the circumstances. At the very least, these verses remind you that God has been with you from the beginning and He isn't going anywhere. He's going to keep pursuing your husband, the perpetrator of this sin, and He's going to keep pursuing you, the victim of the sin. He loves you both with an everlasting love, and He's after restoration for both of you.

> My frame was not hidden from you
> > when I was made in the secret place.

When I was woven together in the depths of the earth,
   your eyes saw my unformed body.
All the days ordained for me
   were written in your book
   before one of them came to be. (verses 15–16)

I see how He knows every single thing about me. He made me, and He knew how I would respond to Mom's illness. Nothing surprised Him in the least. In fact, He was counting on those reactions from me, because He knew He could use that fear and my predictable responses to draw me into His arms tightly again.

"All the days ordained for me were written in your book before one of them came to be." To know that God knew the day of Mom's death beforehand was a great comfort. Her terminal cancer wasn't an accident. She didn't die because I lacked faith or because God lacked love for me; it was part of God's plan.

The overwhelming message throughout Psalm 139 is that your Beloved knows you down to your minutest detail. He knows how you will respond to hard circumstances, whether it's the death of a loved one or the death of a dream with your husband because of sexual sin.

God knows these things before they happen, and He knew how you would respond to your husband's betrayal before it happened. In fact, from the foundation of time, God knew exactly who would be living on earth this very day, and He even knew how many women would be walking this painful road with you this year. He knew that the hearts of many Christians would grow cold to His ways and that many Christian men would be too distant from Him to stand purely in this sensual time.

Since nothing surprises Him, nothing should strike fear in your heart. Remember, as sin abounds, grace abounds even more. He knows you, and He is with you. He will carry you through to the end. Make this truth yours.

> How precious to me are your thoughts, O God!
>> How vast is the sum of them! (verse 17)

My thoughts were always going in the wrong direction, like fixating on what might happen to Mom in the future or believing that God wasn't trustworthy and, therefore, didn't care a whit about my welfare. My thoughts were simply out of line.

But this was a verse I could offer back to the Lord in prayer: *Lord, Your thoughts are the precious ones. Help me learn Your thoughts and how You think about me and what You think of this situation. Show me what is possible for You to do through it all. I do not want to dwell on my thoughts and my old ways of seeing things because my thoughts are not right. Your thoughts are right. Make my thoughts like Yours.*

No prayer could be more useful when life is turned upside down and your thoughts can get so twisted. Because your husband's betrayal was cruel and heartless, he can seem sickening to you. Because his male sexuality is so different from yours, it can seem vulgar. Because his sin is so easily passed to your children, he can seem like an enemy in your eyes.

But thinking that way would be giving in to *your* thoughts, and those thoughts are not right. In the realm of God's precious thoughts, your husband is not sickening and he's not your enemy. If you hope to restore your marriage, you must first restore your heart and fill your mind with the precious thoughts of God.

> Were I to count them,
>> they would outnumber the grains of sand.
> When I awake,
>> I am still with you. (verse 18)

The nights get long when you're enduring unintended journeys as heavy as these, but this verse is your reassurance that He is with you at all times. Best of all, when He goes with you through that long, rough night, He is still there with you the next morning.

On numerous occasions, Fred would get up in the middle of the night and pray over me until the spiritual battle subsided, and then he'd climb back into bed and go to sleep. In the morning he'd be off to work before I woke up. I didn't mind his not being there when I opened my eyes. He left the house at daybreak because he had a heavy workload on his shoulders.

But God never sleeps. When you wake up in the morning, He's smiling, watching over you and looking forward to spending another day with you, protecting you, growing you, holding your hand, and reassuring you. Give him your hand.

> If only you would slay the wicked, O God!
>> Away from me, you bloodthirsty men!
> They speak of you with evil intent;
>> your adversaries misuse your name.
> Do I not hate those who hate you, O LORD,
>> and abhor those who rise up against you?
> I have nothing but hatred for them;
>> I count them my enemies. (verses 19–22)

As I began transforming my mind, learning the right thoughts and maturing the way my Father wanted me to mature, I was aware that a spiritual battle was being fought over me. In fact, spiritual warfare surrounded everyone involved in Mom's terminal illness.

I took these verses to mean that I should direct my anger and hatred toward Satan for all the pain he caused—and not blame God. It all goes back to when Satan successfully tempted Adam and Eve to sin in the garden; the consequences of their sin include death. As Hebrews 9:27 says, everyone is "destined to die once," and that included Mom.

Search me, O God, and know my heart;
    test me and know my anxious thoughts.
See if there is any offensive way in me,
    and lead me in the way everlasting. (verses 23–24)

Oh, my goodness! This passage spoke to my heart so much. The verse implies surrender, and because of my lack of trust, my anxious thoughts and worries, and how close I came to turning my back on the Lord, I can almost feel the tears of David as he cried out, *Lord, search my heart. I don't want to hold on to these things any longer. They aren't right to begin with, Lord, but it's more than that to me. Whatever it is in me that has been in the way of our intimacy, let's get rid of it. I want You to help me to understand my thoughts and where they are wrong. Show me, Lord, so that I can fix them. I don't even know all of my offensive thoughts, but You know everything about me and everything about my innermost being. If there is any offensive way in me, let me hand it over to You. My heart is all Yours, Lord! Search me.*

David ended the psalm with another prayer: "Lead me in the way everlasting." As I meditated on this last prayer, I learned to trust the Lord as David trusted Him, with a full heart of love. With a prayerful attitude in my heart, I said to the Lord, *I trust that You will lead me in the way everlasting, because You aren't just my Lord, Jesus. You are my Friend.*

GAINING FREEDOM

After reading and studying this psalm twice a day for several weeks, you'll have it practically memorized. As God's Word transforms your mind, you can believe that He actually leads you in a different way. You may find yourself praying, *Lord, don't take away my circumstances if that's going to keep me from becoming all that You want me to be. Lord, lead me in Your ways! I've now tasted what You have for me, and what Your abili-*

ties and strengths can do in my life, in spite of my terrible weaknesses. I greatly desire You and Your ways above every other thing, even if it means going through my present hardships.

If your husband refuses to repent and continues to crush your heart through his sexual sin, Psalm 139 will enable you to pray, *Lord, lead me in Your ways, even if it means I can't have my husband anymore and even if I'm forced by his sin to leave this life behind. Whatever it comes to, I have learned through Your Word to see Your strength, and I trust that You can lead me through the hardest and darkest of times.*

In chapter 4, I told you that from the time you first discover your husband's sexual sin, there's absolutely nothing more important than establishing whether you're going to trust the Lord, regardless of the circumstances. Every single thing in your life will hinge upon this question: *Do I trust the Lord, or do I not?*

Once you establish that you do, you have a new priority: memorizing and meditating on Scripture. These disciplines must become the most important priorities in your life, because only Scripture can transform your mind and reveal attitudes and thoughts that aren't right. Only Scripture can restore your heart so that you can grab on to faith in your circumstances and have the peace to live above them. In the midst of an unintended journey, there's nothing more valuable.

7

Worship and Prayer

Polling organizations regularly cite the high percentage of Americans who consider themselves to be Christians and the low percentage of those who actually read their Bibles or know what Christians believe. The percentage of those who worship the Lord at home, one-on-one, must be even smaller. For most of my life, I couldn't number myself among those worshipers either.

To be fair, I can't recall ever hearing a sermon on the topic of personal worship, though I've been a Christian all my life. I *have* heard plenty of sermons on this topic from Fred, but I never understood what he was saying. Nor did I pay much attention to what he did after rising early and walking downstairs to the basement, where he paced back and forth while he quietly sang along—he didn't want to wake me or the kids—to the hymns and praise songs barely audible on his stereo. He'd beat a path across the basement carpet for about ten or twenty minutes, and then he'd kneel for about ten minutes of prayer time. His passion for Jesus grew greatly during those early morning times, and his worship times grew stronger and stronger over the years.

I knew what was he doing down there in the basement at 6:00 a.m. because we talked about what he was learning and experiencing in the Lord. I heard him explain himself once by saying, "Brenda, there's so much more intimacy with the Lord at home than what I find in worship at church. When I'm worshiping one-on-one at home, I'm there for one thing and one thing only: I want to tell Jesus that I love Him, and I want to touch His heart in a way we both long for." Fred explained that since he desired to sing straight to Him from the deepest, most passionate corners of his heart, he preferred worship songs that were sung in second person, songs that were essentially prayers set to music. "Some of these I sing to my Father, and some I sing straight to the Son," he said.

Nodding and smiling, I understood what he meant by second-person love songs. If you were singing straight to Jesus, you would naturally choose songs with the pronouns *You* and *Your.* But Fred didn't stop at my nod of understanding. He wanted so badly for me to catch what he was experiencing that he shared several of those songs with me. One of his favorites, "Destiny" by Chuck Dennie, goes like this:

I'm found in Your love
I want to run into, into Your beauty

Another one, "And I Worship" by Monique Tute, includes these words:

I will worship You my love
For taking every stain I wear

After playing these songs, he asked me a bold question. "Do you sense the yearning and the passion for intimacy with Jesus in them?" he wondered. "They have almost a romantic feel to them, like the kind of love songs a man might sing to his girlfriend or wife."

He wanted me to *experience* what he was experiencing with the Lord, that romantic side of worship, that connection with Jesus that can be so electric and passionate. I didn't get it for the longest time. Do you experience this kind of passion with the Lord when you tell Him you love Him? Or is it more of a run-of-the-mill experience on Sunday mornings? For me, it was more like the latter. To be honest, I also felt that Fred was just one of those favored children of the Lord and that's why Fred got to experience some things that I didn't.

When Mom suddenly became ill and we learned of her terminal condition, however, a tsunami of pain washed my world away right down to the foundation, and I clung to His truths like a drowning woman might cling to a floating log. One of those truths is that the Lord loves me and He doesn't love anyone else any more than He loves me. Since I was now beginning to believe that truth with all my heart, I could no longer pass off Fred's experiences as something only for the "favored ones."

Perhaps that's why I finally caught what Fred was saying when I read his chapter on worship, "Experiencing the Father Through Worship," in *Tactics* and then began pursuing the Lord in worship with a very personal focus in the privacy of my home. Shortly thereafter, I had an amazing breakthrough in my intimacy with the Lord while worshiping with Fred one night before bed. He was lying on the floor of our master bedroom, listening to the music and singing away as usual, and I was curled up in a chair in the opposite corner, trying to stay warm. Out of the blue, my heart began to swell with an impassioned love for the Lord, and I heard myself murmur, "I love you, Jesus!"

Instantly, I realized that I couldn't recall ever saying anything like that to the Lord in my life. Oh, I may have said something along the lines of, *I love You, Lord, You are so good,* but I'd always refer to Him by His title, Lord, rather than the more personal "Jesus."

Not this time. On this occasion, I called Him by name, and I expressed my love openly to my Beloved. It was such a shocking, cataclysmic shift in my heart that my voice was shaking as I called across the room, "Fred, I just told Jesus I love Him for the first time."

"What did you say?" Fred asked. I could sense the surprised confusion in his voice. What I uttered was such a shocking admission that Fred leaped to his feet, stopped the music, and flipped on the lights to make sure he had heard me right. Like me, he was completely dumbfounded but also thrilled out of his mind.

Sometime, somewhere during Dad's dying days twenty-five years earlier, I had locked my heart away from Jesus and His lovely touch. All that time He'd been trying to work His key back into my rusty old heart, and He'd finally managed to trip that lock. Worship just exploded in my life, adding a deeper degree of closeness with the Lord on top of everything else I was learning about Him. Worship was no longer a one-way performance for some distant King sitting on His throne. This was one-on-one interaction with the One who passionately loves me.

THE GREAT REWARD

Until I got it, I never fully realized what the Lord means in Genesis 15:1 when He calls Himself my "very great reward." I'm certainly grateful I get it now. Whether your life is hitting on all cylinders or you have broken down somewhere on an unintended journey, your one pursuit, your one reward, must be Jesus.

Perhaps you're on an unintended journey and pressing into God, asking Him to move into your life with His power and blessing to fix your mess quickly. Believe me, I understand the sentiment perfectly. Tomorrow couldn't be soon enough!

Still, His answer isn't the main issue, because having things answered your way isn't your great reward. Whether He answers your prayer instantly or seems to put you on hold, Jesus is the One you live for. As long as you've been drawn closer to Him in the process of prayer and worship, you've gotten your reward, no matter what the outcome.

He is your great reward.

WHY PRAYER WORKS

Before worship began to explode in my life, I experienced a deep hunger to find out exactly what prayer was. I wanted to know how it worked and why it worked.

More than that, I desired to understand the intimacy of prayer and how to make it permanent. I was so tired of being out of touch with Him during my day. I would pray and have my devotions in the morning, but because I'm not a morning person, I often fell back asleep.

Even when I did manage to keep my eyelids open, I found that I seldom connected with the Lord again in prayer for the rest of the day, which started really eating at my heart. I knew that I needed to take the Word everywhere with me—written on my handy note cards—if I expected the truth to have the transforming impact that I longed for. I also realized that I needed to be in touch with Him personally throughout the day if I expected to handle everything being thrown my way.

I began to pray two things for myself:

1. that I would understand prayer and what is going on in prayer
2. that His Word would be at the tip of my tongue in prayer, and that I would learn how to use His Word in prayer

I decided to begin praying for five minutes at the top of every hour. I didn't get legalistic about it. If I forgot one hour or I missed it because I was doing something else—like driving or enjoying dinner with my family—I let it go and waited until the next hour. But I was very committed and very creative, so if I possibly could, I would stop whatever I was doing for those minutes in order to focus completely upon prayer. For instance, if the big hand hit twelve when I was in the pool during my swimming workout, I'd simply switch from the front crawl to the kickboard, and I'd pray as I kicked along the top of the water. If I happened to be showering at the club after getting out of the pool when the top of the hour came, I'd pray while I soaped up.

I usually spent the whole five minutes in prayer, but sometimes I spent it in worship—if I wasn't in a public place like a fitness-club shower room. The deeper you go in prayer and intercession, the more worship and prayer blend together. They are practically inseparable, as both are intricately tied to your intimacy with Him. That was exactly what I was after.

My little top-of-the-hour system worked beautifully, although some hitches developed. For one thing, I had evidently burst brightly onto the Enemy's radar screen the moment I began. If you decide to try something along these lines in your prayer life, expect an intimidating response from the Enemy—he wants you to stop.

During that first week, Fred and our daughters, Laura and Rebecca, were each attacked viciously in their spirits. It was as if in the midst of the Enemy's dark, cold world, my prayers had flipped on a piercing laser beam directed toward heaven, and he was rushing about in a panic, trying anything to snuff out the light.

But I wasn't about to flip it off again. He may have the power to intimidate me, but I know he doesn't have the power to destroy me or my family. Those intimidating strikes were simply signs that I was on the right track, and besides, they gave me another opportunity to believe God in the face of tough circumstances.

Rebecca's hit came straight out of left field. She had been preparing to head back to her dorm at Iowa State that Sunday afternoon when she suddenly fell into a deep, disturbing, and inexplicable funk about returning to school. The darkness in her face and eyes was extremely uncharacteristic of her normal bright, sunny disposition, so different that I was quite troubled and concerned. I called her after she'd left home to make sure she'd arrived at her dorm safely, only to discover that her mood had worsened significantly.

As I hung up the phone, I glanced at the clock and noticed the time. It was the top of the hour. Good! I thought to myself. It's time to pray anyway! The Lord wasted no time revealing that Rebecca's mood was the result of a spiritual assault that the Enemy was using to get me to back off on prayer. Joy bubbled in my heart, in spite of this news. This was exactly the kind of tighter communion with God that I'd been hoping to find as I stretched out my prayer time to cover my day.

Rushing to find Fred, I clued him in on Rebecca's situation, and we were soon kneeling shoulder to shoulder in prayer, returning fire on the Enemy's attack upon our daughter. When I called Rebecca an hour later, she was back to normal, her bubbly voice as spunky as ever.

When you become a giant, irritating blip on Satan's radar screen, you can be pretty certain you're doing something right in the Lord's kingdom, but when the Lord Himself begins to deliver extravagant answers to your prayers, every doubt will vanish.

During that same week, for instance, the Lord firmly rebuked Rebecca twice on her attitudes toward the body of Christ, something Fred had been speaking with her about for a couple of years. She had watched her beloved sister, Laura, get torn apart by her youth group at church, only to be crushed herself when her youth pastor was convicted of sexually abusing Rebecca's friend—and doing it while on a mission trip, of all things. Rebecca's cynicism toward Christians and their facades had been building for several years, but inside that first week of expanding my prayer life, Rebecca was so heavily convicted by the Spirit—twice—that her change of heart was immediate.

In fact, the Spirit suddenly became quite active in all our lives. All of our children called with reports of their own increased communication with God and further growth in Him even before they'd heard about the changes I'd made in my prayer life.

So what's going on these days? I've resisted Satan and he has backed off, just as the Bible promises, proving once again that God's Word is true in my life. As for the Spirit, He's still quite active, and God is answering my prayers on a regular basis. Don't get the wrong picture here, however. That doesn't mean I'm getting the huge, flashy answers every week like the one we had with Rebecca, and you shouldn't expect those answers regularly either. After all, I'm like everyone else. Most of the time, there just isn't that much going on around here. I'm making beds, running errands, fixing supper, and driving kids around.

But that's okay. I don't need the flamboyant or the flabbergasting to keep my faith high or to keep me praying. Remember, His answers are not my great reward. My Lord is my great reward, and whether or not life is moving fast or crawling slowly around here, my intimacy with Him is now deep and precious. That was what I was after from the beginning, and that is what I urge you to chase. That is all that matters over time.

Not long ago, Fred asked me if I'd noticed that God was delivering on His great promise to me, the one He'd made to me when I was still offended with Him. The Lord began pursuing me in that dark time, and while I couldn't fully respond to Him, He still offered me a special blessing if I would just let go of Mom's hand and take hold of His. Perhaps you recall the promised blessing at the end of the message He delivered to me through my friend Sandy:

He promises that…you will learn an unshakable dependence on Him that you have never fully realized before. This will also drive you to a higher level of prayer to which you have been called but in which you have not walked consistently, a level that is beyond anything you've known or understood before.

If you remembered this promise (from chapter 4), you're doing better than I did. I had completely forgotten that promise in the midst of my stress, and I certainly wasn't thinking about it when I made my decision to pray at the top of every hour.

But Fred hadn't forgotten it. He had that promise in writing, and as he quietly watched the Lord methodically and deliberately restore my heart and my mind, he was always on the lookout for a sign of that promised blessing blossoming in my life. Fred was now seeing those indications, and the Lord was seeing all that He'd hoped He'd see in me on the other side of this unintended journey.

FROM FRED

What does praying Scripture do to the Enemy? It disorients him. Using the Word in prayer against the Enemy is like cracking him on the head with a baseball bat. While I'm not certain that Satan sees stars, he does see churning chaos all around him as his head begins to spin. Why does it happen this way? Think about the Enemy's spiritual environment for a moment. Humans live in an environment of air, and fish live in a cool, watery environment. What makes up the environment in the spirit realm? Answer: authority and rank. Every move made and every breath taken happens within the context of authority and rank.

Now think about Jesus. He is the incarnate Word of God, inseparable from the Scriptures. When you use Scripture in battle, you are standing in the authority of Christ, almost as if you are costumed with Jesus's royal clothes. The Enemy can't see your puny little self or hear your squeaky little voice spouting off scriptures. In that environment, all he can see and hear is the authority and rank of Jesus.

It's as if Jesus Himself is towering behind you with his arms crossed and His steely jaw set. His authority dominates the environment. When your Enemy hears Scripture in your prayer, he sees Jesus, and he's frightened out of his pants, just as the demons were when Jesus confronted them in the Bible. When Jesus spoke to them, it never even occurred to them to argue with the Lord, not for a nanosecond. In their environment, that didn't even make a bit of sense. The only thing that did make sense was to get into begging-for-mercy mode. His authority was too much for them. He was the undisputed champion, the highest authority in the spiritual realm.

What scriptures do you use for spiritual warfare? I especially like the psalms in the Old Testament. When David brought up his enemies before the Lord in prayer, he asked God in harsh, direct terms to chop them to ribbons. We can't pray that way against our earthly enemies anymore, of course. Jesus has given us a new command, to love our enemies and to pray for them.

But that doesn't mean we can't take on David's attitude when it comes to our spiritual enemies. I think God expects that from us, and I do it all the time. Let me offer my favorite battle scripture as an example:

> His heart is secure, he will have no fear;
>> in the end he will look in triumph on his foes....
> The wicked man will see and be vexed,
>> he will gnash his teeth and waste away;
>> the longings of the wicked will come to nothing.
>>> (Psalm 112:8, 10)

Now see how I take up this scripture as my weapon and personally hammer the Enemy with it, reminding him what the end of the game will look like:

> *My heart is secure, and I have no fear of you, Satan; in the end,*
> *I will look in triumph on my foes, and that means you too.... You,*

the wicked one, will see me standing in victory, and you will be vexed. You will gnash your teeth and waste away. Remember all of those longings you have to be like God? One day, they will come to nothing.

Before I go on, I want you to know that I've always learned far more by practicing prayer than by reading about it. In fact, the books are often most valuable for explaining the things I'm already experiencing in practice. You, too, will learn a lot more about prayer by doing it than by reading about it.

Still, before I turn you loose to pray, I'd like to paint a quick picture of how I approached the spiritual-warfare prayers in the dark days after Gwen's diagnosis. As Brenda mentioned earlier, I began fasting from all food every other day and heading over to the Blue Chapel of Prayer at my church every afternoon. As far as I was concerned, I was fighting for Gwen's life.

On one of those days, the Lord asked me to give Psalm 139 to Brenda. On that same day, He asked me to begin praying Psalm 140 daily on Gwen's behalf. So I inserted her name and her pronouns into this psalm and prayed it like this:

Rescue Gwen, O Lord, from these evil demons that would kill her mercilessly with lung cancer; protect her from these demons of violence who devise evil plans in their hearts and stir up war with my mother-in-law every day. They make their tongues as sharp as a serpent's, and the poison of vipers is on their lips. They rise up and mock You, Lord. They think they will pay no price for doing this to her. Teach them a bitter lesson, Lord.

Keep Gwen, O Lord, from the hands of these wicked ones and protect her from the demons of violence who plan to trip her feet. These proud enemies have hidden a snare for Your daughter Gwen, and they have spread out the cords of their nets and have set traps for her along her path, to kill her, right under our noses.

O Lord, I say to You, "You are my God." Hear, O Lord, my cry for mercy on Gwen's behalf. O Sovereign Lord, You are my strong deliverer. You shield our heads in the day of battle—do not grant the wicked their evil desire to kill Gwen, O Lord; do not let their plans succeed, or they will become even more proud and arrogant in their slimy, dark world.

Let the heads of these enemies who've surrounded Gwen be covered with the very trouble their own lips have caused. Let the demons writhe in cancerous pain. Let burning coals fall upon them. Throw them into the fire and into miry pits so that they may never rise again. Let these demon slanderers never be established on Gwen's land, which is Your land too, Lord. Instead, hunt them down with withering disasters of their own making.

I know Your promises, Father. I know that You secure justice for all of the poor and needy in this world, like Gwen. You always uphold their cause. Your Word promises that the righteous will surely praise Your name, and I'm absolutely certain that Gwen, being righteous in You, will always live before You to give You praise.

But Lord, please let her live before You here, on earth. Let her praise Your name from here, with us. Take away her cancer, and let that healing bring You the glory You deserve, even as she stands arm in arm with us, praising Your holy name.

As I prayed, I would remind Satan and all his minions that they would one day be thrown into the fire, never to rise again, and that I would be praying for disaster to hunt them down incessantly. I also reminded them that even if Gwen were never healed, she would stand before the Lord as His righteous one, and she would be forever praising

His name no matter what they did, whether she was living before the Lord here on earth or living before Him in heaven.

Prayer always has its effects in the spirit realm. The only thing you must remember is this: It won't be the one who reads about prayer who will move mountains, and it won't be the one who believes in prayer who will cast that mountain into the sea. It won't even be the one who aches to pray more often who will carry the day in battle. It'll go to the one who prays.

You need to pray, my friend.

8

Believing God

From Brenda

Pat Ashby, my counselor, gave me some crucial advice early on. "It is vital to watch your self-talk, Brenda," she said. "Your thoughts will determine your feelings, and your feelings will determine your behavior. That's why it's so important to examine your thoughts. You see, you can't change your feelings directly, but you can change your thoughts." Pat had the right idea, as this scripture attests:

> We demolish arguments and every pretension that sets itself
> up against the knowledge of God, and we take captive every
> thought to make it obedient to Christ. (2 Corinthians 10:5)

I had seen the power of this verse in my husband's life during his battle for sexual purity, but how do you capture thoughts you don't recognize as wrong?

At first, the wrong thoughts racing through my mind were so common that I had trouble recognizing them as wrong when they flashed by. I'm talking about thoughts like, *I should be able to go to Mom's appointments without breaking down,* or, *I should be able to see Mom without wanting to run away all the time.* The only time I got some help was when I'd sit with Fred and verbalize some of these thoughts. He was great at spotting those *shoulds* and reminding me what Pat said about thoughts determining your feelings and feelings determining your actions. Once I learned to recognize these thoughts as they came in, I could finally begin a conscious effort to capture, dump, and replace them with the truth of Scripture.

This is where the book *Believing God* by Beth Moore became so helpful. Aptly titled, it teaches how to believe God and to replace wrong thinking with the truth. Beth presents a five-statement pledge of faith that gives me a specific way to practice taking up my shield of faith in the heat of battle. These five statements define the bigger concept of believing God:

- *God is who He says He is.*
- *He can do what He says He can do.*
- *I am who He says I am.*
- *I can do all things through Christ.*
- *God's Word is alive and active in me.*

According to Beth, it didn't matter what kind of wrong thoughts came bustling through my mind, because at least one of these five statements could shoot them down. If a panic thought rushed into my mind—*I can't be here with Mom right now*—I could replace it with the fourth thought listed above: *But I can do all things through Christ who strengthens me.*

If I happened to think, *Everyone must think I'm rotten,* I could replace it with: *But I am who God says I am: His beloved, the apple of His eye.* Beth's excellent teaching sped up the transformation process dramatically for me.

I read from Beth's book every day as part of my devotions. I would read one chapter a day, slowly—underlining, highlighting, making notes, meditating. When I finished the final chapter, I flipped back to chapter 1 the next day and started over again. I was desperate to learn and be reminded how to trust God for what He had planned for me, not just for everyone else. Packed with Scripture and packed with truth, Beth's book was every bit as critical to my growth as any other of my spiritual disciplines.

Beth Moore also taught me the importance of journaling. She pointed out that one of the key jobs of the Holy Spirit is to remind us about what we have already heard from the Lord:

> Without a doubt, memory is a vital part of the learning process, and it is also a vital part of the faith-building process.... As Christ prepared His disciples for His absence, He gave them this assurance:
>
> "But the Counselor, the Holy Spirit, whom the Father will send in my name, will teach you all things and will remind you of everything I have said to you" [John 14:26].
>
> When you and I received Christ, the Spirit of God took up immediate residency inside of us. He has many roles, but one targeted in this verse can be most involved in the task before us. The Holy Spirit is the blessed Reminder. He can as easily remind us of what we've experienced with God as He can remind us of what we've been taught. (Nashville: Broadman & Holman, 2004, pages 179–80)

If the Holy Spirit chooses to make these reminders priorities in our lives, we ought to make them priorities in our spiritual disciplines as well.

Perhaps the idea of writing down what God is teaching you is something you've never heard about. Or perhaps you've heard about journaling but have never gotten around to trying it. Either way, I strongly suggest you give it a go.

When you're under the stress of an unintended journey, Holy Spirit reminders are critical to your growth. Don't take the Lord's lessons for granted. They'll fly away like birds, because you'll be prone to lose what He's already taught you. The last thing you want to do is rob yourself of the encouragement that a review of His revelations can bring to you, so make the effort to write down what you're going through in a personal journal.

TRAUMA VERSUS ETERNAL GLORY

> We are hard pressed on every side, but not crushed; perplexed,
> but not in despair; persecuted, but not abandoned; struck down,
> but not destroyed.... Though outwardly we are wasting away,
> yet inwardly we are being renewed day by day. For our light and
> momentary troubles are achieving for us an eternal glory that far
> outweighs them all. So we fix our eyes not on what is seen, but
> on what is unseen. (2 Corinthians 4:8–9, 16–18)

Was the apostle Paul waxing eloquent, or can you expect these fine words and godly observations to be true in your life as well? I certainly can't claim with certainty that my troubles achieved very much in the way of eternal glory, but if you were to ask me whether or not my trauma was worth something to me because of what I gained in this present life, I would answer without question, *Yes, it was absolutely worth it.*

I'm most thankful that the Lord loved me enough to work all this out in me now, here on earth. It would have been crushing for me to arrive in heaven and finally have the opportunity to look into His beautiful eyes, only to hear Him say, *You never trusted me!*

I encourage you to seek personal intimacy with Him with all your heart. Get busy with Him, and He will get you through your unintended journey. His gentle rebukes are precious, and His encouragement endearing.

As I close my portion of this book, let me remind you that when it comes to unintended journeys, questions will always remain. My big question is, why did both of my parents die at such relatively young ages? I still have no idea why the Lord took Dad when he could have had such a huge impact on Fred and our young marriage, nor can I explain why He took Mom when we needed her so badly. But while the questions about my parents' deaths will always remain, I have learned to stop asking them. God is God, and I am not. It's just plain silly to think for one second that I'm always going to understand His mind and His plans. That's why I don't worry about those things anymore.

Mom's death no longer looks like a betrayal to me. I've learned to accept that bad things happen in this world, so now my aim is to find God's grace and strength in the midst of incredibly difficult situations.

These are a few of the permanent lessons I've learned on this unintended journey, though I must admit I'm not too anxious to experience another one real soon. Half of me is afraid of getting a D on my report card for the way I handle the next one, in spite of my new understanding. But I'm not going to sweat it too much. After all, I flunked the last time, so even a D would have me moving in the right direction!

No matter what grade I get the next time, the following passage, which I read dozens of times before my unintended journey, has taken on new meaning for me:

> Consider it pure joy, my brothers, whenever you face trials of many kinds, because you know that the testing of your faith develops perseverance. Perseverance must finish its work so that you may be mature and complete, not lacking anything. (James 1:2–4)

Though I've been a Christian all my life, I had never believed that pain and joy could coexist. That's changed now. Though my pain never stopped from the day of the cancer diagnosis to the day of Mom's funeral, I was staggered to find a pure joy bubbling up in me anyhow—a joy impervious to everything else I was going through—born of the certain knowledge that the Lord was right there with me in my circumstances.

I was no longer offended by God. Everything was as it should be, and everything in my life lined up with what I knew about God. I chose to transform my mind through spiritual disciplines, just as He had called me to do (see Romans 12:2). The power of His Word spawned a miraculous freedom in my life, and the glory of this victory was all His, just as it was supposed to be:

> The Lord is the Spirit, and where the Spirit of the Lord is, there is freedom. And we, who with unveiled faces all reflect the Lord's glory, are being transformed into his likeness with ever-increasing glory, which comes from the Lord, who is the Spirit. (2 Corinthians 3:17–18)

His reflected glory shines from the pages of my journal. Since Mom died in June, January through June marked the second half of my final year with her. As you read through these entries, take a look at His wonderful work in me. See how He delivered on His promise to show me a place of blessing above my circumstances. See how He restored my heart even before my unintended journey was over.

January 6

I'm being hammered to learn to trust the Lord and to have faith in Him. I was reviewing today's verses, and I noticed something I hadn't noticed before in Jeremiah 17:7–8: The man who trusts in the Lord and has confidence in Him will not fear or worry. What a great reminder of the benefits of trusting Him! Thanks, Lord, for this revelation.

January 29

The secret to being transformed is learning to wait on the Lord and quiet our souls before Him. That's how we'll be changed.

February 5

If you want to learn to love Him, focus on God's love for you and what He's done for you. This causes the river of living water to flow in your life. Don't strive to love Him. Just focus on His love for you.

February 27

How can I face the rest of my life without Mom? When I've thought about this before, I've often felt I would lose my mind with grief. But today is different. The Lord has encouraged me by showing me that I'll handle the future just as I'm learning to handle everything else right now—just one day at a time, or even one hour at a time. I need to be careful not to grab the pain of my whole future without Mom, not to focus on the whole thing at once.

I read this today in one of Corrie ten Boom's books, and it encouraged me too: "Always when I say that I am not able, I get the same answer from the Lord. He says, 'I know you can't. I have known it already for a long time. I am glad now that you know it for yourself, for now you can let Me do it.'"

March 26

Sometimes when I'm tired spiritually, I know I need to rest, but I need to rest in God, not from God.

May 6
    I grieve over the loss of what will never be because of Mom's dying. But I will be watching to see how God can turn these losses for His gain.

June 19 (funeral, end of day)
    This was the day I've dreaded. One of my early thoughts today was, One more hard thing left to get through, and it's the hardest one of all. But I was able to have a good amount of time early today for devotions.... God's grace was sufficient for this day, and Mom would have been so proud. It was a day that honored her in every way and one that honored God in every way.
    We drove to the cemetery, and it was very sad to see the coffin sitting there. We all took a flower out of the arrangement on the coffin.... Still, I didn't experience the awful, harsh grief like I did with my dad. There was a grace underneath, a deep strength from the outside.

I'm still quite human, of course. Painful thoughts still manage to fight their way into my head from time to time. Fred is still playing his role for me, reminding me of the same old things over and over. Still, in spite of my imperfections, the Lord has proven Himself awesome in battle once more, and my love for the Him has never been more emphatic or more passionate. Here are some words from Fred's journal:

August 31
    Today Brenda told me, "I visited Aunt Barbara at the hospital today, and she told me that Brian and

Shelly were taking their girls to the circus this weekend, and it really stabbed me. This is Labor Day coming up. We should have had tickets to see that circus
with Mom, just like we did every year over Labor Day.
Remember how she used to pick up coins on her walks
throughout the year and use that money to buy circus
tickets?"

Chuckling, I nodded. "That was so much like
Gwen!"

"Anyway, after I left the hospital, I thought about
how I'd failed everyone last fall, and how I lost us so
many memories we could have had—one last time
at the circus, one last trip to Ledges State Park, a few
last trips to the Amanas—we could have really had
a great autumn while she was still feeling pretty good,
but I failed all of you."

"You didn't fail anyone, sweetheart," I told her.
"Failure implies that you had a choice, but you had
no choice. You collapsed. No one knew how your dad's
death had affected you and that your trust in God was
a house of cards. You didn't fail anyone. You simply
collapsed.

"Besides, success and failure can't even begin to be
discussed outside a time line for context," I continued.
"Even if you insisted on calling that collapse a failure,
it was only a failure in the short term. When I look
back at it, all I see is the long-term victory, the re-
markable display of hard work you put in to restore
your heart, and the stunning rally that snatched
victory back from defeat. I don't see a loss at all. That
collapse was just the first quarter of the game. You

finished so well, and the last six months were great and filled with a ton of good memories."

"It's funny, Fred," she marveled. "No matter how hard we try as Christians and no matter how good we become as His children, we're going to hit patches of failure. But look at how faithful Jesus was! He was and is always faithful, even when we fail. How could anyone not want to have a relationship with Someone like that!"

Part 2

Susan's Unintended Journey

9

I'd Rather Not Be Here

It is a certainty that you aren't reading this book for your pleasure. To say that you would rather not have a need for this book, that you would rather not be here, is undoubtedly an understatement. I understand the deep desire you feel to simply eradicate your present situation. But the distressing reality is unchangeable. You may have just learned that your husband deceived you. Perhaps you have uncovered some painful truth and have a gnawing suspicion there could be more underneath. Possibly you have been enduring betrayal in your relationship for many years and are ready to confront the circumstances in a fresh way.

Maybe your instincts tell you that things are not right, but you feel you have no grounds to speak up. Maybe you fear you're in a troubled marriage, unable to trust in your spouse's integrity. Perhaps you find yourself feeling jealous as your partner eyes another. Maybe there is a feeling of disconnect when you are together and you're missing true soul intimacy. Yet no matter what the situation, *you are not alone.*

As much as you may feel alone in your distress, millions of women are experiencing the same pain, attempting to navigate through what appears to be uncharted territory. Yet regardless of whether you have discovered a one-time affair or a long-standing relationship with pornography, prostitutes, or an individual, the path to healing is the same. And determining if your marriage is salvageable is found on a similar journey.

No doubt you did not expect this when you entered your relationship, or you at least hoped against it. Nonetheless it has intruded, an unwelcome reality, bringing a deep sense of betrayal that has left you reeling. Your mind and emotions may be leading you on a journey that has you going in circles, reviewing your relationship's history and obsessing over the betrayals, vacillating between anger, hurt, and denial, only to be led back to the same place you began. And then starting all over again.

My goal in this section (and in the guidebook) is to lead you to a better place. You don't have to be stuck here. You will find more information than you might have expected and people who understand your circumstances. Avenue ministry provides the resources for you to find peer support and the right direction to heal from sexual brokenness. I like to think of the Avenue program as a true compass to guide and lead you along the path of tangible healing.

And above all, it will instill in you a hope for your future.

In fact, I know how much you'd rather be somewhere else because I have been where you are. In 1994, after twelve years of living in a marriage punctuated by pain-filled moments, the truth finally came out. There were no places to hide anymore from the truth that had been hidden behind secrets or lies, and it seemed there was nothing but more unfathomable pain ahead of me. The truth about my husband's double life inflicted indescribable wounds, heartache, anger, and resentment.

I had no idea what I needed to heal, but God did. And after a while, I realized He had prepared a place for me. A few years before the bottom fell out of my world, He brought my husband and me close friends, other couples we could trust and confide in, for the first time in our marriage. Through those friendships, I found a community of women who understood what I was going through. For the first time as an adult, I experienced the fulfillment of being in the company of women.

After the bomb dropped, those women were there to listen to me vent my feelings and encourage me with the truth of God's love. They prayed for me and with me. I came to realize that close, intimate relationships, so new to me then, were a vital component of the healing process of every woman. Those experiences were the foundational cornerstone of the healing I now offer to you.

We are all unique, each of us experiencing our own degree of pain and depth of wounding, depending on our personalities, our histories, and our husbands' particular behaviors. Yet no matter what the details of what you have suffered, the wound is the same.

Questions

Among all the questions that swirl in a woman's head at this time, the two most weighty are: *Should I end the marriage?* and, *How can I stop the pain?* Each of those questions is a catalyst for an endless barrage of more questions. Though dwelling on the questions can cause angst, realize that the reason they're stirring is because they need real answers.

Most women faced with this kind of turmoil in an intimate relationship ask these questions in silence, ashamed and insecure. At the core, that shame is fueled by the big question asked by every woman who faces this sort of situation: *Why aren't I enough for him?*

The answer to that is multifaceted, but the reality is that it may have nothing to do with you. If your husband is trapped in sexual sin, he may be seeking to soothe his own internal struggles and numb painful emotions without making that connection or understanding the real reasons himself. He may be continuing on a detrimental path he learned years ago. We'll delve into the whys of his actions in a subsequent chapter.

If you're in this situation, you may be plagued by a flood of other tormenting questions as well:

- *Has he told me everything?*
- *How can I ever trust him again? Would I know if he was at it again?*
- *Why can't I stop thinking about what he did?*
- *Why didn't I see this coming? How could I be such a total fool?*
- *How can he make me feel so inadequate?*
- *I can't stand the sight of him. How could I feel love for him again?*
- *I can't tell anyone; how would they understand if I stayed?*
- *If anyone knew, I'd die of shame. How could I tell anyone?*
- *How can he be so together in other parts of his life?*
- *People think he's such a great guy; what if they knew?*
- *How could he do this to me, after everything we've been through?*
- *How can I leave…with two children, and one on the way?*
- *Can I trust him with the kids?*
- *How can I hurt him like he has hurt me?*
- *Why do I think like this? Sometimes I wish he were dead.*
- *I can't even move from my sofa. How can I move from my depression?*

Though questions like these may plague you right now, I sincerely hope that shame over your circumstances does not keep you from moving forward through this book and the guidebook. They will help you find the answers, and you will learn how to make healthy decisions, how to act upon your concerns, and how to find healing for your difficult emotions.

PSALMS

If you are anxious about all the questions you're asking or embarrassed by your own thoughts, I'd like to thrust the book of Psalms into your hand and say, "Read."

Psalms is literally bursting with the inner questions and emotions of people who have had their share of trouble. The psalms are surprisingly gritty, full of words spoken to God by others who were livid with anger or weighed down by depression. Some people find their own feelings reflected in these passages and use them as their own prayers. You may find this helpful, especially if you don't have much energy to muster right now.

God is not afraid of your emotions. He already knows what's going on inside you. He knows your fear, your anger, and your shame.

> Lord! Help! Godly men are fast disappearing. Where in all the
> world can dependable men be found? Everyone deceives and
> flatters and lies. There is no sincerity left…. The Lord replies,
> "I will arise and defend the oppressed, the poor, the needy.
> I will rescue them as they have longed for me to do." (Psalm
> 12:1–2, 5, TLB)

Don't believe the lie that you are not able to approach God with your anger and grief; that is completely missing the message of Christianity. God knows us, and He wants us to come as we are, to sit with Him in our brokenness so He can comfort us. Only He holds the answers to help you trade in your shattered ruins for hope, joy, and freedom.

Try reading a few psalms as you start out on your journey here, and don't fear being honest with God. We'll come back to this thought in a while.

For now, I want to share with you how I first started asking these questions in my own life.

10

This Isn't How
I Pictured My Story

This is not the marriage I envisioned. Just like every woman who looks forward to being married, I had a picture in my mind of what I hoped my marriage would be like. And there was no page in my mental photo album for sorrowful images.

Eventually, we all learn that forging a life with another is not as picture perfect as the image we dreamed of. However, the unwelcome pain I came to endure in marriage rendered the image completely indiscernible.

There is a part of me that dislikes reexamining this old album, because I've moved on. I've already analyzed every ugly detail, and I don't live in that pain anymore. Even the faded memories of those excruciating circumstances aren't pain filled. They are faded, but they are not altogether forgotten.

Yet I now view this page of my album from a broader perspective. I hope reading the details of my experience may be helpful to you and others—maybe to someone who has never spoken to anyone about her pain as she tries to make sense of what is happening in her life.

Note, though, that I do not believe that every woman in this situation came from a troubled home, and early family experiences do not necessarily contribute to the state of a woman's marriage. In my conversations with thousands of women, I have seen that many things influence our lives and our spouses and that no single factor can account for these things. While the aftermaths share many similarities, no instigating situation is exactly the same.

CHILDHOOD

My early childhood home was fairly average for the era I grew up in: Mom stayed at home to raise six children. My dad was successful in his career. We lived in suburbia, and my siblings and I attended Catholic schools. We went on nice vacations each summer. My dad was moderately involved with us kids. We ate dinner together each evening and went to Catholic Mass every Sunday.

I remember only one loud fight between my parents when I was a youngster, but in my teen years, arguing became almost a nightly event. My mother was searching to find new truth in the spiritual realm—she immersed herself in the study of reincarnation, psychic phenomena, numerology, and astrology. She attempted to indoctrinate our family in her latest discoveries. My father had no tolerance for her new beliefs or anything he disagreed with. Eventually my Mom rediscovered Christ with a deeper understanding, but my parents continued to spend most evenings arguing spiritual versus religious doctrine.

During that same period, my father started having "a cocktail or two" each evening. He was short-tempered when sober, and the fuse quickened after his drinks. He became physically violent with my mother on numerous occasions. My sisters, brothers, and I were on the receiving end of his anger when we'd get up the courage to speak our minds. And often he'd shame us when we didn't know an answer to one of his intellectual challenges.

So as a teenager, I learned to lie low and keep my mouth shut. My siblings and I were tightly bonded, but I don't remember talking about these experiences and our fractured emotions. I vowed that no man would ever lay a hand on me in anger. What I didn't guard myself from was the less tangible but palpable emotional abuse I experienced at the hands of my father.

My mother protected neither herself nor us from that harm. She threatened to leave my dad but never did. She had her own childhood wounds that she had not overcome and passively allowed the cycle to continue. As her marriage became more troubled, she became more emotionally unavailable. My mother took good care of our physical needs, but she was ill equipped to raise teenagers. She offered us no guidance in understanding the onset of puberty, and alternately hurled shame at my sisters and me when faced with that parental responsibility. It was the way her mother had handled it. Her motive was love and a desire to keep us out of harm's way, but her methods denied any discussion.

My parents labeled me the easy one. My quiet demeanor masked my deep desire for attention and my unmet emotional needs. Compounding the problem, I was allowed to date at the tender age of thirteen. Clueless about situations I ended up in, I didn't have much internal fortitude to head off boys' advances. And once I experienced being special, I soon felt incomplete without a boyfriend.

Although I had no lack of boys pursuing me, I didn't see how my desperation for acceptance caused me to hang on one guy after another, always waiting for a better one to come along. Fear of my father's wrath definitely helped me draw boundaries, but mostly it motivated me to keep secrets.

The only well-delivered and informative advice I got about boys came from Ann Landers' newspaper column. One thing she said saved me from losing my virginity at a very early age. Paraphrased, it read, "Boys will try to score with you and then lose respect for you. Then they are off to the next conquest." That was the best counsel I received. It stuck with me, and I am thankful for it.

The tension in our home continued to escalate, and I made a plan to move away from home as soon as I turned eighteen. Armed with basic office skills, I easily got a job to support myself. I looked very together on the outside, but inside I was a needy mess. I was attracted to boyfriends who had a strong work ethic. No hippies for me. I was barely nineteen when I married, which my mother was pushing me to do because I was already living with my boyfriend. My father, on this rare occasion, sat me down for a talk—not once but twice—advising me that I was making an unwise decision.

The Cycle Continues

My fiancé was generally happy and easygoing, but he revealed another layer of his personality after I started living with him. He would have angry outbursts triggered by some frustration, and I would retreat into my lie-low posture. Fear gripped me. I didn't sign up for this, but I was more afraid of being alone. It made no logical sense. I was reasonably pretty and had no lack of opportunities to date. I could provide for myself, but still I was not willing to risk being alone. The very thing I disrespected in my mother, I was now becoming.

After we married, my husband's anger didn't go away but got worse and was usually directed at me. Although he never laid a hand on me in anger, he would hurl objects across the room, smashing a phone one time, another time a chair. I walked on eggshells, never knowing what might trigger the next explosion.

I never spoke to anyone about his temper. Why did I make this my shame and not reveal my painful world to anyone, not even my mother? This was my mother's *normal* existence, so I figured, what could she offer? Without even realizing it was happening, I disconnected from school and work friendships. I abandoned church, as it didn't seem to offer any relevant help to my life. In fact, it had the potential to create even more disharmony, just as it did in my parents' relationship, since my husband considered himself an atheist. I created my own isolation, and I never even thought about why.

We were married for two years when I got pregnant, despite being on the pill. We excitedly told family and friends about our expectancy, but from the moment I received the news from my doctor, I went into depression at the prospect of becoming a mother at the age of twenty-one. I thought of my mother's life, and I saw how trapped she'd become in her unhappy marriage by the responsibilities of motherhood. I looked into the newly legalized option of abortion and discussed it with my husband. He left the decision up to me. A sense of immense relief washed over me, and my depression lifted. I intended to tell my family that I miscarried.

I went into the doctor's office for a preparatory procedure the day before the abortion was to take place. Upon arriving home that evening, my husband broke down in tears, expressing his true feelings. He really wanted this baby. It was a gut-wrenching night of honesty we'd never experienced before. I agreed not to go through with the abortion, and I called the hospital that night to cancel. But the nurse on the line told me I had no choice at this point, that I would probably miscarry because of the dilation procedure and have life-threatening complications if I didn't follow through. She stated as a matter of fact, "You can always get pregnant again."

In my whole life, I have been in no deeper pit than at that moment. I felt I had no one to talk to. I broke the news to my husband, and after a wretched night, we robotically did what had to be done in the morning.

After the procedure, as I lay in the cold postop room with a handful of other women, I broke into uncontrollable tears and sank to a new depth of depression. The shame and loss were unfathomable. My baby and I both bore the consequences of my fears.

After that day, my husband and I never spoke of it again. We went into our own personal silences of mourning.

Less than a year after the abortion, my husband came to me to confess a brief affair. The woman he got involved with and her husband were our friends. Ironically, she was newly pregnant with their first child. My husband wanted to clear his conscience, but his idea of "housecleaning" was to sweep all the emotion and broken pieces to my side of the room. I was now burdened with a new shock and grief. I wanted to talk about it, but he said, "Get over it or leave." I tried, but I didn't know how to forgive and forget. So I merely checked out emotionally, continuing in the marriage for the same reason I married in the first place—fear of being alone. Part of me knew it was just a matter of time before I'd leave this painful marriage.

CLAY

Another year later, I ventured into a new career, and it was there that I met Clay. After getting to know each other as colleagues, we became friends, which led to flirtations and eventually my initiating a full-blown affair. Like my husband, Clay was also very ambitious and a hard worker. In other ways that were very important to me, he seemed so different from my husband. He wasn't hot-tempered and was extremely romantic, gentlemanly, and sophisticated. I decided to separate from my husband and deceived myself that I was finally getting the backbone to take care of myself. The reality that I couldn't see was that the only reason I was able to leave was because I felt secure in the relationship I was now in with Clay.

Clay and I moved in together. We had an exclusive relationship, although there was no talk yet of engagement or marriage. I treasured the honeymoon feeling I had and couldn't imagine that the future would be anything but rosy. But after we lived together for about a year, odd circumstances aroused my suspicion. Both our work schedules often involved evenings working with clients, but for Clay some evenings went much later, and he would not commit to being home at any specific time. One evening Clay returned after midnight and unknowingly gave me strong evidence that he had been involved with someone that evening. I interrogated him, but he assured me that nothing was going on. I desperately tried to convince my heart, but my mind knew what it knew and would not be quiet. I found myself battling my own denial. I didn't want this garbage; I wanted what I had believed Clay was. Again fear took hold, and I couldn't walk away from him because of my own insecurities.

Rather than look reality in the face and break it off, I started looking at myself to fix the things wrong with me. I began what was to be a decade-long pursuit of perfection. But no matter what I did, in Clay's eyes I never measured up. I was never thin enough; I didn't dress sexy enough in public; I wasn't aggressive enough in bed.

SEEKING HELP

We had lived together about a year and then, steeped in denial, I became engaged to be married to Clay. The engagement was a security blanket; I wasn't really ready to marry. I stated that I'd like to wait about two years. During our engagement, I became suspicious again of Clay's behavior and confronted him with evidence. This time he confessed to visiting a prostitute on two occasions. He broke down in tears and confided that he felt he had no self-control over his actions. He said he wanted our marriage more than anything, he wanted to be my knight in shining armor, and he would never do anything to hurt me like this again.

I felt like I had been hit in the stomach. I wrestled between wanting to kick him out and wanting the security of being married. I said I needed some time and a separation. "How long?" he begged. Ultimately, my desire to take away his anxiety overrode my own need to separate. I went to a counselor instead, and the outcome was worse than having not gone at all. The only therapy this learned counselor offered was to scream and throw a tissue box across the room to vent my anger.

I told Clay I forgave him, but the reality of his behavior now overshadowed everything in our relationship. I walked into this marriage just like I had my first, with a gnawing feeling in the pit of my stomach that I was making a mistake and trying to hide the truth from myself and everyone around me. We had many wonderful moments in our marriage, and there were still things I loved about Clay. But my reaction to being betrayed was the same as it had been in my first marriage: I found sex to be stomach churning and revolting. I recoiled and felt like I would wretch at any intimate touch.

About a year into our marriage, I uncovered new evidence that Clay was at it again and had also lied about how often he had visited prostitutes prior to our marriage. I was despondent, and my first instinct was to run—fast. But I contemplated that here I was at twenty-eight ready to bail on my second marriage. I decided I needed to try to deal with the problem.

I insisted to Clay that we get counseling. We ended up with another counselor who did not have a clue about compulsive sexual behavior. Unbeknownst to me, this counselor told Clay in private sessions that his behavior was perfectly normal. During our sessions with her, I would attempt to drag the truth out of Clay. My husband was not forthcoming about the full extent of his actions and would continually try to change the subject to financial woes. The counselor would go along, following Clay on any rabbit trail he chose to divert the discussion away from the real problem. I wanted to scream with the frustration.

For a short season, I began wearing provocative clothing in public to satisfy Clay's requests. What used to be admiring glances from other men now felt more like gawking and leering. Though a part of me delighted in turning heads, I eventually came to realize how much I was devaluing and degrading myself, so I decided I needed to leave Clay to keep my sanity and dignity. I rented a small cottage and spoke with our counselor, expecting her to encourage me for facing my fear, but she believed I was acting on my fear by running away. So I stayed.

We continued to go in circles in our counseling sessions. In the end, another counselor turned out being worse for our marriage than no counsel at all.

REBIRTH

After this, Clay's addiction went completely underground. I stopped finding signs. Yet his attitude toward me was increasingly intolerant. He always said I had a "vivid imagination" and he wasn't doing anything, but he would use the opportunities of my interrogations to say he was tempted because I was so unattractive. This dance went on for the next seven years.

In 1990, at the age of thirty-six, something started stirring in me, and I finally chose to listen to that small voice. I had shut it out for so many years, but I had come to a new place in my life. I didn't know what was going to happen to my marriage, but for the first time, I was truly willing to risk. I decided that I needed to do what was necessary for *my* life.

First on the list was to find God again. Turns out He was waiting for me. When I walked into a church my sister had told me about ten years earlier, I immediately knew I was home. After that, I started taking care of myself in new ways. I stopped starving myself, and I found walking more enjoyable than spending all my free hours in a gym. I reassessed my career. I refused to submit to Clay's suggestions to dress provocatively in public. I stopped obsessing about what Clay might be doing. I asked God to show me what I needed to know and stopped playing detective.

During that time, I wasn't changing Clay, but I had a new peace that was, as they say, beyond understanding. It wasn't denial. I knew what that felt like. This was letting go and being willing to trust God to make whatever changes I needed in order to walk His way.

Because of all the arguments about religion in my childhood home, I didn't even hint to Clay that he attend church with me, but within the first week, he asked me about the church and said he would like to go with me the following Sunday. That was the beginning of a new journey in our relationship. We attended every week, and we both had a rebirth.

That's not to say that all was well. Clay had a full-blown addiction to sexual images and was still struggling to control his illicit behavior. I was still unaware of the facts, but I felt in my heart that something wasn't right with him.

In this new environment, God brought both of us a gift that we didn't even know we needed. Friends. Real friends. We were inundated with people He orchestrated for our life. I discovered honest people who spoke openly about the real-life problems and trials in their relationships. Previously, my adult friendships centered on having a good time on the weekends, which is not to say these new friends were lacking in the fun department. We started with fun get-togethers, but those relationships revealed their depth and strength as time progressed.

It was three years later that Clay first talked seriously about the prospect of starting a family. A part of me desired to become a mother, but I thought it was unconscionable to bring a child into a marriage that had such unresolved problems. At that point I said I couldn't entertain the idea further until he got real with me about his secrets. Astonishingly, he confessed many behaviors he had been engaged in during our entire marriage. He confessed to having provocative phone calls with prostitutes as a masturbation tool and paying for oral sex. Oddly, I felt a sense of relief that I wasn't crazy all those years with the vivid imaginings Clay accused me of.

But as days wore on, I sensed I did not have the full truth from him, because his confession didn't address old incidents that still nagged at me. I gave him numerous opportunities to tell all, and he assured me he had made a full confession. I felt we needed to seek counsel with a pastor at our church.

The church turned out to be loving, gracious, and helpful. The pastor prayed with Clay and was insightful to include specific prayer to release him from any demonic oppression that may have been a catalyst to this confessed habitual sin.

But beyond prayer, he offered Clay no direction for overcoming his ingrained habits or my hurts. I was still left with an unsettled feeling I couldn't resolve. I had nothing to go on but my own gut feeling, and I was so used to not trusting it that, once again, I brushed the feeling aside.

STARTING A FAMILY

For the first time in my life, I shared my confidences with a few good friends. They had shared experiences from their own lives with me recently, and that opened the door, as I knew there would be compassion. They encouraged me, prayed with me, gave me a place to cry, and gave me hope and strength. There was no judgment, no religious dictates to follow.

Clay and I went forward with trying to conceive, and within a few months we were expecting. After our daughter was born, we were both elated and overwhelmed, as all new parents are. I was busy mothering and running my business. Clay continued to work long days, six days a week, but at least now that we were churchgoers, he took Sunday off.

Our daughter was six months old when Clay again began to experience stress about our finances. He had been doing ample business, but it seemed every time he needed to write a check, there was not enough money in the account. I went to the office and went through all the bookkeeping, starting with the checkbook. In short order, I discovered that a new employee to whom Clay had blindly handed over the checkbook had embezzled over seventy thousand dollars within two short months.

She was immediately arrested, and I was left to clean up the mess. Fortunately, in the bigger scheme of things, I uncovered another fraud. Phone bills revealed the same pattern I had uncovered years before. It laid bare evidence that Clay was up to his old ways again. By this time I knew that God was in the details; although the embezzlement was a nightmare, it was also an answer to my prayer: *God, show me the truth about Clay, and if there's deceit, please reveal it to me.* He did.

This time I knew what I knew, and I was not sitting still for half confessions. I told Clay to keep his distance. I needed to sort out what had to be done for myself and our child. Clay wallowed for a week or so until something broke within him and he knew he had to tell all. First he went to a few of his good friends and spent the evening telling them all the sordid details of the last year's destructive behaviors and lies. To his astonishment, he experienced the hand of Jesus that night: no condemnation—only love, encouragement, and strength to do the right thing.

The next day he told me the whole truth. This time his confession was akin to a dam bursting. In sharp contrast to his previous deceit-speckled fragments of truth, Clay finally confessed what he wasn't willing to before. One lie unconfessed left a stronghold for the Enemy of his soul to latch on to and have a field day. Although Clay had gone through a prayer of deliverance, God couldn't deal with what was not revealed.

His secret was not so much worse than the others, but for him it was a personal boundary he told himself he would not cross, a secret he believed he could lose me over. And in his mind, it was unforgivable. It was an encounter with a woman we both had worked with years before. He had compartmentalized his other behaviors, and in his mind, this one was the deal breaker. That became his nemesis: by holding on to the secret when given the opportunity to release it, Clay allowed the subsequent year to consume him with one-night stands. The more he acted out, the more he sank into his own personal loathing and depression.

Although he did what he knew he had to do by telling the truth, he also knew he was going to risk losing things he held dear—his marriage and a full relationship with our new baby daughter. But he knew he had to let go of trying to control the outcome, although he didn't know how I would react to this reality.

Again I felt vindicated; I wasn't crazy for being jealous with vain imaginings. But that knowledge didn't help me overcome the intense emotions I experienced. I was faced with the ugly truth that Clay had been unfaithful in one form or another throughout our marriage. My initial reaction was shock. It began with a deafening, numbing paralysis and quickly elevated into anger. I got very quiet for what seemed like an eternity to Clay. My mind was racing. My first words were, "How could you do this to me?" I felt the full fruition of my worst nightmare—I was trapped in a rotten marriage for the sake of my child. Every fiber of my being wanted to be rid of Clay forever and punish him by taking away every legal right to be with his child.

What followed were weeks of deep grief interspersed with more anger. But the two crucial issues that lay before me—my personal healing and putting our marriage back together—were two separate and distinct issues. I knew they had to be. I needed to move forward to take care of myself, be emotionally stable, and be a good mother in the midst of this storm. I was at such a different place in my life now. Here I was with a child to care for, and yet for the first time in my life, I wasn't afraid to be alone.

I knew I had the inner strength to be without Clay. But there was also another part of me that had strengthened over the previous five years. I was willing to hear from God and follow His lead. I had made so many wrong choices doing things my way, figuratively putting my hands over my ears and running headlong into destructive decisions that I deeply regretted, all out of fear that God would not provide for me. I knew that I had every biblical justification to leave the marriage. But I made a decision in those first few days that I would listen intently for God's voice and direction and would go His way.

THE POWER OF FRIENDS

That decision was easier to make than to keep. My emotions were like waves in a storm, and in my decision to stay the course, I felt like a ship challenged to stay afloat on that very stormy sea. One moment I would despise Clay; another moment I'd feel compassion for him. My best friends became my lifeboat in those moments.

One friend in particular made herself available by calling me every day. Sometimes, depending on my state of mind, the phone call felt like a welcome rescue. Other times I wanted to be left alone, to ignore my condition or drown in my sorrows. Nonetheless, I would always take her call.

She would coax out of me how I was doing, and I found myself venting how I really felt as she listened patiently. She offered compassion and understanding. She, too, had been through betrayal in her marriage. She offered me hope and wisdom. She always seemed to have the right words to encourage me in the place I was most desperate. She always ended our conversations by praying for me, and she didn't advise me or expect me to have it all figured out.

Having friends who loved me in spite of the mess was a gift far more precious than anything else I could have received. I trusted they would remain good friends whether I stayed married or not. Instead of wearing masks and keeping it all looking good on the outside, each of us was able to talk about our failings and sorrows and know that we would not be judged or talked about behind our backs.

I felt that the direction God was giving me was to wait and see. He wasn't expecting me to trust Clay, but He also didn't want me to run. At first I felt I wanted and needed a separation during the wait-and-see period. Clay started looking for a temporary place to call home.

But in a matter of days, I felt that I would be just as comfortable with an in-house separation. I could see that Clay was contrite about his past behavior and was willing to give me the space I needed. He was willing to be accountable for his time and his whereabouts.

Staying together under one roof only worked because Clay had surrendered to God. He was accountable to other men whom he stayed tight with while he began his walk toward a new way of thinking and living. I didn't own Clay's problem, and I wasn't trying to fix him. I had stopped needing to take care of him before taking care of myself.

At times when hurt and grief overwhelmed me, I would hold my daughter. I prayed for God's protection over her spirit, soul, and body. She provided a physical and emotional comfort for me as much as I gave the same to her. I could not receive any physical or emotional comfort from Clay. It was so tainted.

LISTENING

During this period of in-house separation, I listened fervently for God's voice to give direction. I had put my trust in Him instead of in Clay. I went for daily walks in our neighborhood, baby in tow, spending time talking with God in between talking and singing to my daughter.

During one of these walks shortly after Clay's confession, I told God that I was willing to forgive, but I didn't really know how. I told

Him that I had no feelings of forgiveness, but that I was doing so out of my desire to do His will. I asked God to show me how to forgive and to take away the feeling of hatred. I knew that I needed to forgive Clay whether or not we reconciled.

One day as I was praying, my life began to replay before me. I felt as if I were seeing video clips of times my actions were an affront to God. Some I had long forgotten and never felt any real remorse for. Other memories still held the stinging pain of shameful regret. In those moments, God gently helped me remember my own sin. I realized that I never even asked His forgiveness for most of my behavior, because at the time I did those things, my mind and heart were turned away from God, and I was living my life on my own terms. In that encounter with God, I confessed those things that grieved God's heart, and I asked His forgiveness.

I was humbled by the reality of it all. Some of my behaviors had impacted Clay and may have contributed to his behavior. Some of my regretful actions hurt other people earlier in my life, and I needed to seek forgiveness from them. But in this moment, God was shining a spotlight on how much He had forgiven me.

God was answering my prayer to show me how to forgive Clay, but not in the way I expected. He gave me the best incentive to forgive Clay: forgive him as God has forgiven me. That whole experience took the wind out of my sails and quieted my internal questions of *Why me?* The following months I stayed steady on this course, allowing God to do new things in my life and fix things that needed repair.

I had no way to know if Clay's repentance would be a lasting change. But I kept my eyes wide open, seeking truth about my circumstances. I knew God would take care of my daughter and me, regardless of the choices my husband had made or would make in the future. God gave me a hope for my own future, and it wasn't based on the outcome of my marriage.

Watching Clay's attitudes and behaviors transforming before me, I saw a gradual process making him into a new man. He was no longer secretive. Instead, he was willing to talk about his daily struggles. He stayed tightly connected to other men who were striving for the same open qualities in their own lives. He stayed submitted to our new pastor's counsel, going through a weekly session together with a few other men to deal with his longstanding compulsive behaviors. He was willing to answer the myriad questions I had for him, filling in the blanks from years of lies.

As months progressed, he opened up to other men about his struggles and his victories. This depth of communication was missing several years before when he made his incomplete confessions. Back then he did not talk about his issues, even though I expected him to, knowing his personality. A born salesman, Clay usually makes sure everyone hears about something he's excited about. This time he became the megaphone for other men who were dealing with the same issues. This was tangible evidence of real change.

As I waited upon the Lord and waited to see whether Clay had changed, God was also softening my heart. He showed me that what causes divorce is not just the failings of husband or wife but a hardened heart of one or both of the spouses. As Clay was going through this transformation, which included a new heart, I was softening the hard shell I had formed around mine to protect me from being hurt again. There were also hard layers of anger and bitterness I had to continually be mindful of. Although our personal journeys of healing were not complete, I made a decision to renew our marriage. This wait-and-see period lasted about six months, although I had no set time line in mind at the beginning. My decision to stay married was grounded on what God showed me about forgiveness and renewal.

When I thought of what Jesus felt when He was betrayed by those closest to Him, I knew I had only an inkling of how He overcame His personal grief to extend forgiveness to those who didn't deserve it and to offer His hand in love again to those who had failed Him. I was humbled. Jesus was fully human, but with the mind of God, He knew that His actions would affect people's lives for eternity. God had given me a glimpse of how He hopes we respond to betrayal. I came to realize that my actions would have an impact on others as well.

MINISTRY

I didn't have a ministry in mind when I first thought about how my actions could have an impact on others' lives, but I knew that my decision couldn't be just about me. My father left and filed for divorce when I was twenty-three. I saw my parents' divorce have a devastating effect on our family. In fact, my parents' divorce gave me permission to divorce my first husband. There had never been a divorce on either side in my parents' family histories, but in the few years after my parents divorced, six other divorces occurred within our extended family. My two young brothers' lives were littered with the debris of our parents' divorce. Looking back, I am convinced that we became vulnerable to a spiritual influence that carried enormous power to take down marriages and leave the carnage of shattered dreams in its wake.

With that knowledge weighing on my heart, my first priority in my decision was the welfare of my daughter. Her father was a new man, but would I stand in the way of keeping our family intact because I wouldn't forgive? I also felt a deep burden not to let the Enemy of my soul have another victory in my life. If I walked out, he would win again. My decision was based not on my emotions but on following Jesus's lead. I didn't desire to be a martyr, but in order to overcome the betrayal, offer forgiveness, and create renewal of relationship, I had to suffer.

My suffering was mostly about confronting and surrendering my pain, protectiveness, and pride. Many times I had to wrestle with the desire to flee. Over and over again I had to remove the veil of the former man that I kept draping on Clay's face. A thousand times I've had to climb over my protective wall to become physically vulnerable and intimate. I've been shocked by the retorts from my own lips that didn't miss an opportunity to fling poison darts filled with sarcasm and laced with bitterness, revealing what was hiding in my heart. My journey to a fresh start could have been less painful if I had been able to crucify all my destructive emotions and protective stances in one fatal act.

If Clay hadn't died to his old ways, my decisions would surely have been different. But we were both new creations, with God as the designer. So the questions came down to these: Was I willing to allow a resurrection of our marriage? Was I willing to let God have the victory? God gave me the choice, and I wanted to choose well this time.

Through this darkest storm in my life, as I drew close to God, He stayed with me every step along my unintended journey. I allowed that rain to wash away the decayed debris in my life. Then God used that debris to nourish the ground, to grow new things.

> My beloved said to me, "Rise up, my love, my fair one, and come away. For the winter is past, the rain is over and gone. The flowers are springing up and the time of the singing of birds has come. Yes, spring is here." (Song of Solomon 2:10–12, TLB)

God didn't settle for just keeping my marriage intact. He birthed *many* new things in my life, including a better understanding of His heart for me. He took away the sting of the painful memories. He helped me love my husband with a new kind of love. He showed me how to take my dependence off my husband and put it in Him. He showed me how much He grieved for our circumstance. He showed me that how I respond to my circumstance is of immense importance to Him. He's teaching me to concern myself less with what others think of me and to dwell more on what He thinks of me. He has released me from the bondage of fear.

He allowed me to face my worst fear and find Him in the process, showing me that my pain and emptiness was what drove me back to Him.

When I rededicated my heart and my life to God back in 1990, He gave me a desire to serve Him. I found my niche when I became involved with the seasonal decorating of the church. This was work that I was comfortable with, as my profession was interior design. I filled that role for about seven years. I enjoyed making things pretty, and I always appreciated hearing how the decorating lifted people's spirits. I picked that ministry, and God blessed others through it.

But God opened up another door and asked me to enter. This ministry was not of my choosing but an acceptance of God's invitation. It felt like the opposite end of the spectrum, rubble instead of pretty things. But God has shown me a thousand times over what He can do with piles of messy rubble when we bring them to the Master Builder.

The following scripture was offered to me by a friend as *my scripture* when I first stepped out in faith to offer my hand to other women who were trapped in the place where I once lived. I believe these words are the calling for every aspect of the ministry God named Avenue. As you read this, I hope you recognize and soak in the promises God is speaking over you, the very woman He wants to heal and set free.

> The Spirit of the Lord God is upon me, because the Lord has anointed me to bring good news to the suffering and afflicted. He has sent me to comfort the broken-hearted, to announce liberty to captives and to open the eyes of the blind. He has sent me to tell those who mourn that the time of God's favor to them has come, and the day of his wrath to their enemies. To all who mourn in Israel he will give:
>
> > Beauty for ashes;
> >
> > > Joy instead of mourning;
> > >
> > > Praise instead of heaviness.
>
> For God has planted them like strong and graceful oaks for his own glory.

And they shall rebuild the ancient ruins, repairing cities long ago destroyed, reviving them though they have lain there many generations.... You shall be called priests of the Lord, ministers of our God.... Instead of shame and dishonor, you shall have a double portion of prosperity and everlasting joy....

His righteousness shall be like a budding tree, or like a garden in early spring, full of young plants springing up everywhere. (Isaiah 61:1–4, 6, 7, 11, TLB)

11

Sticks and Stones

Remember that childhood saying "Sticks and stones may break my bones, but words will never hurt me"? It's a snappy retort on the playground, but it doesn't offer any real defense. Words can hurt. A lot. Long after a bruise heals, the taunting words of the school bully continue to ring in our ears. When we don't challenge the wounding words of other people and our own thoughts, fears, and pride, we set ourselves up to be easy prey to our spiritual Enemy. But God has given us strong weapons for combat and the ability to gain victory in the war for our minds.

> Though we walk in the flesh, we do not war according to the flesh. For the weapons of our warfare are not carnal but mighty in God for pulling down strongholds, casting down arguments and every high thing that exalts itself against the knowledge of God, bringing every thought into captivity to the obedience of Christ. (2 Corinthians 10:3–5, NKJV)

We are to take captive every thought that enters our minds and weigh it against the truth of God's Word. If it doesn't align with what

God says, we need to bathe in His words to renew our minds and flush out the poisonous dialogue. When we refresh our thinking, our spirits and souls are in tune with God's power to overcome the things that otherwise have the ability to take us down.

Every word of God is pure;
He is a shield to those who put their trust in Him.
(Proverbs 30:5, NKJV)

The destructive words of others and our own negative thoughts, if left unchecked and internalized, can create strongholds in our lives. Looking back with twenty-twenty hindsight, I see that by not employing God's protection to eradicate destructive ways of thinking, I sent myself down a long detour, away from the good things God had placed along the path He had chosen especially for me. I can't tell you exactly what God had desired for my life those years, but I know the life I was living was not by His design. I did not know, much less understand, the principle of taking thoughts captive. Consequently, I was an easy target for the Enemy's lies and the unloving words of those around me.

This spiritual Enemy is in a war to win a particular territory: your mind. Look at verse 5 in the 2 Corinthians passage on the previous page: it refers to dealing with arguments, knowledge, and thoughts. These all happen in the mind. If you can be sucked into believing what the Enemy wants you to believe, he has won the first battle. He first persuades you with lies, and then he is able to provoke you into unhealthy actions based on your faulty beliefs. If you can be convinced of a lie about yourself or a lie about the possibilities for your future, the Enemy has begun to create a stronghold by which he can block you from understanding God's promises for your life.

When this occurs, you may develop a sense that you are powerless to take control of your life, and this feeling wreaks havoc with your ability to recognize that you are, nonetheless, the coauthor of your decisions and your emotions. The result: you've allowed things into your life that you really didn't want because you were clueless about the power available to you to make positive choices.

The power of destructive thoughts is crystal clear to me now. Looking back, I realize I had an experience that changed me profoundly. I remember learning about men cheating on their wives at age twelve. I was in a car with my mother, and she was carrying on about all the men in the neighborhood, including my dad's golf buddies, who were unfaithful to their wives. She proudly proclaimed that my dad always came home right after golf on Saturday, unlike the other golfers who stayed to drink and meet up with their mistresses. I remember that very moment gave birth to a profound fear that I didn't know how to prevent ending up with a husband who was unfaithful. It seemed inevitable, although it was something I surely did not want.

My father left and filed for divorce after thirty years of marriage. He had been unfaithful at various times throughout the marriage. That reality added cement to my negative belief. I was gripped and controlled by the fear that my husband would be unfaithful.

I know in my heart of hearts I would have been happy to be in a loving marriage with a guy without issues. But I was one of the walking wounded. I was raised by a father who never made me feel cherished and a mother who didn't know how to nurture a child past adolescence. I had been exposed to the realities of the fallen nature of humanity and feared that I would be incapable of captivating a man's heart to win his faithfulness. The result of those experiences left me emotionally needy; I had a personalized set of luggage filled with issues that caused me to end up weighed down and stuck in situations that I didn't want but didn't know how to change.

You probably recognize negative patterns that repeated themselves throughout my life. I was not living by the 2 Corinthians scripture just mentioned. Instead, I was living life based on a foundation of flawed wisdom and beliefs that led me down destructive paths to regrettable choices. My mistakes could be summed up like this:

- I didn't seek godly wisdom.
- I learned to be silent on important matters.
- I chose to smother my instincts.
- I made my decisions from fear.
- I didn't value healthy friendships.
- I dismissed the need to take care of my emotions.
- I dismissed the need to have God in my life.
- I didn't trust that God wanted His best for me.

I didn't invent this kind of flawed thinking. It started in the Garden of Eden. The Enemy went after Eve rather than Adam because he hated Eve's beauty. She was the human incarnation of the beauty of God. Before Adam and Eve arrived, Lucifer lived in the garden. It was his domain. He was perfect in beauty and full of wisdom. He was breathtaking. But his own pride in himself was his undoing.

> Son of dust...the Lord God says: You were the perfection of wisdom and beauty. You were in Eden, the garden of God; your clothing was bejeweled with every precious stone.... I appointed you to be the anointed guardian cherub....
>
> You were perfect in all you did from the day you were created until that time when wrong was found in you.... Your heart was filled with pride because of all your beauty; you corrupted your wisdom for the sake of your splendor. Therefore I have cast you down to the ground and exposed you helpless before the curious gaze of kings. You defiled your holiness with lust for gain. (Ezekiel 28:12–15, 17–18, TLB)

Satan was looking for revenge for his punishment. He resented Eve's beauty and wanted to bring her down. He did that with a few diabolically planted words. He put thoughts in her head that went unchallenged. He planted the seeds of doubt that God would give her every good thing. The first woman ever created succumbed to his words, and she adopted distrust of being loved perfectly. She took matters into her own hands, trying to make things happen on her terms, instead of trusting God for His best.

If Eve, who had bodily perfection and no competition, was fair game to the Enemy's lies, how much more susceptible are we? Every woman knows that she is not perfect. Even the most beautiful women privately examine and berate themselves for their physical flaws. Because we know we are not perfect, we are easily sucked into the lies that the Enemy plants in our heads. The wounding words of our husbands carry weight because we know a grain of truth lies there: we *aren't* perfect.

But our lives here on earth aren't about being perfect. In heaven, we will all be perfected. Yet in this life, our greatest calling is to love one another.

Let love be your greatest aim. (1 Corinthians 14:1, TLB)

God loves us fully in our imperfect state. Our husbands are called to cherish, encourage, protect, and love us as we are. Just the same, we are to love our husbands, flaws included. Even with all my own failings, my husband's sins were his to own. Just because I had a skewed perspective did not give him license to betray me. He had to answer to me and to God for his actions

"But I Wasn't Messed Up Like You"

You may have had a lovely childhood and emotionally healthy parents who knew how to express love and encouragement. Perhaps you've walked with the Lord your whole life. You may have done everything right: waiting patiently, choosing well whom to marry, and doing everything you know to please your husband as a wife is called to do. Yet, in spite of all you've done right, you find that your husband has been looking at pornography, engaging in chat rooms, or having an affair.

Our spouses are also susceptible to believing lies about themselves and about God's truth. They are prey to ungodly thoughts. They may be sucked in by fear, by believing they have to take control to get their needs met. They are susceptible to believing that they can live their lives as they choose, by their own rules, and deceiving themselves that they are invincible and will not experience consequences for their actions.

Once they go down this path, the natural human response is to deal with the guilt by blaming someone else for their actions. In this situation, it is usually the wife who becomes the fall guy. If this has happened to you, you have heard hurtful statements from your husband about how you don't measure up as a woman. Some blame is blatant— your husband may disparage you with accusations of lackluster performances in bed to justify his actions. Some blame is subtle, such as your husband taking the blame on himself for having a stronger sex drive than you.

These remarks can create devastating feelings of inadequacy that may have you questioning yourself. If left unexamined, these feelings can sidetrack you into focusing on your husband's list of your shortcomings and distract you from identifying the real problem. Just as my wrong thinking sent me down the wrong path, the same result can take place in your life if your husband's accusations are not brought into the light before God. It is of utmost importance to weigh his words with what Scripture says about the same things.

As wives, we are called to be available and wholeheartedly involved in lovemaking. Still, we need to determine what is *normal* in the bedroom—and that is one of the world's great mysteries. *The Healing Choice Guidebook* will help you evaluate this perplexing dilemma—and it won't look like the latest *Cosmo* quiz. Using biblical principles, it will help you examine the health of your sex life. You may determine that there are adjustments that need to be made on your part. That said, there is no justification for porn or infidelity. And once those offenses have occurred, making healthy changes to improve this area of your relationship is not a simple matter. It becomes part of the much bigger process of reconciliation and healing.

For now, let's look at some of the erroneous thinking that a husband is prey to and the subsequent blame that may have been put on your shoulders.

BEAUTY

He may compare your physical appearance to other women's appearances and determine in his mind that you are lacking something. He justifies to himself and to you that this gives him permission to stray. But look at these scriptures to consider what God thinks about the importance of physical beauty.

> Don't be concerned about the outward beauty that depends on jewelry, or beautiful clothes, or hair arrangement. Be beautiful inside, in your hearts, with the lasting charm of a gentle and quiet spirit which is so precious to God. (1 Peter 3:3–4, TLB)

God loves beauty. God is beauty. He created the beauty in this world and the human form. God made you as you are, and your husband married you as you are. God does want us to take care of ourselves, and there is nothing wrong with bringing out our best with clothing, hairstyle, makeup, and jewelry. What God is saying here is that our beauty regimen is not to stop there. We need to put *more* importance on our inner beauty, our character, than we do on our outward appearance.

God's thoughts on the matter of beauty are in sharp contrast to the lies your husband is speaking to blame you for his lack of self-control.

Has your husband made disparaging remarks about your signs of aging? Maybe you have gained a little weight after birthing several children and things are moving south. What does God think about being faithful to a wife who is no longer youthful?

> Drink from your own well, my son—be faithful and true to
> your wife. Why should you beget children with women of
> the street? Why share your children with those outside your
> home?... Rejoice in the wife of your youth. Let her charms
> and tender embrace satisfy you. Let her love alone fill you with
> delight. Why delight yourself with prostitutes, embracing what
> isn't yours? For God is closely watching you, and he weighs care-
> fully everything you do. (Proverbs 5:15–21, TLB)

IDOLS

Has your husband ever justified his interest in pornography? Has he told you it's no big deal?

> But I [Jesus] say: Anyone who even looks at a woman with lust
> in his eye has already committed adultery with her in his heart.
> (Matthew 5:28, TLB)

Men use visual images for arousal and masturbation. Many men are literally addicted to this behavior, although a wife may have no understanding of the scope of his thought life and no knowledge of his self-serving actions. The purveyors of pornography would have women believe it is a harmless bit of male entertainment. They would have men believe it is a man's indisputable freedom to look at what he wants to gaze upon.

The time will come when men will not put up with sound doctrine. Instead, to suit their own desires, they will gather around
them a great number of teachers to say what their itching ears
want to hear. They will turn their ears away from the truth and
turn aside to myths. (2 Timothy 4:3–4)

When a person idolizes what God created, he has created his own
god. Obsession with pornography fits that model of idol worship with
precision.

They exchanged the truth of God for a lie, and worshiped and
served created things rather than the Creator. (Romans 1:25)

CAPTIVES

Use of pornography typically drags a man into further thoughts of sexual activity, into other forms of sexual compromise.

Don't lust for their beauty. Don't let their coyness seduce you.
For a prostitute will bring a man to poverty, and an adulteress
may cost him his very life. (Proverbs 6:25–26, TLB)

In each situation the man's thoughts have led him into these places
because he was not taking every thought into captivity. The world we
live in has strong influences that would lead us down destructive paths.
We are called to test what the world is trying to sell us, using the Word
of God.

Do not conform any longer to the pattern of this world, but be
transformed by the renewing of your mind. Then you will be
able to test and approve what God's will is—his good, pleasing
and perfect will. (Romans 12:2)

Without that unchanging guide to give him wisdom in all aspects of his life, a man will be led along like a pig with a ring in his snout to the pigpen and, eventually, the slaughterhouse.

> All at once he followed her
>> like an ox going to the slaughter,
>> like a deer stepping into a noose. (Proverbs 7:22)

A woman is susceptible to being caught in the same snare and led to the same slaughterhouse, although for different reasons. Rather than being led by the nose like a man who has no self-restraint on his sexuality, a woman may purposely become the bait that she hopes will tempt him. Just as I did for a season, millions of women become obsessed about their appearance, attempting to be more beautiful than other women to attract a man or to keep their husbands from wandering. They dress provocatively, constantly comparing themselves to other women.

> A beautiful woman lacking discretion and modesty is like a
> fine gold ring in a pig's snout. (Proverbs 11:22, TLB)

> You thought you could get along without me—you trusted
> in your beauty instead; and you gave yourself...to every
> man who came along. Your beauty was his for the asking.
> (Ezekiel 16:15, TLB)

This desperate behavior is typical of a woman longing to be captivating to a man who will cherish her. A woman with needs unmet, a woman with wounds from rejection, neglect, or abuse, is usually found hiding behind the seductive facade.

Anna Nicole Smith's tragic life and untimely death were a magnified embodiment of this kind of destructive striving. She exploited herself for attention, allowing herself to be consumed by the world. She settled for being loved only for her beauty, and she came to believe that it was the only thing of value she possessed. In spite of her outward beauty, in spite of her fame, in spite of her wealth, she was a sad and lonely woman who numbed her pain with drugs.

EXTREME MAKEOVER

We've all witnessed normal and naturally beautiful people undergoing drastic cosmetic surgery for an "extreme makeover" in the hope of securing the love and happiness that eludes them. If you have been snared by this trap, it is not too late to be rescued and change your course. God is waiting with open arms to embrace His daughter and show her how lovely she is in His eyes.

Do you know why we long to be "enough" for one man? Why we desire to be captivated by the one we love? It's because God wrote that script on our hearts. The youngest girl is enamored with fairy-tale, happily-every-after stories of princesses being swept away by their knights in shining armor.

Women love their chick flicks where it's all put together in the end. We hang on the edge of our seats, desperately wanting the man to find the woman, to embrace her and comfort her with his vow of unfailing love. That kind of love makes a woman feel like a woman. Without it, her soul withers. Without it, she becomes harsh or desperate or depressed.

God wants to give us that kind of life-giving energy, and the best part is that we don't have to wait to be loved like that, whether we're married or not, whether our marriage is peaceful or in a raging storm. God wants to have that kind of love affair with you, regardless of your marital status. If that sounds strange, I assure you it is biblical.

You have stolen my heart, my sister, my bride. (Song of Songs 4:9)

When a woman comes to the place where she is comfortable, assured, and protected in His love, she radiates a new beauty from the inside. I have witnessed many women go through this transformation, sometimes even as their earthly marriages fell apart. I have seen women who were the personification of neediness, anger, or grief reborn from cocoons of suffering. When they took the risk and allowed God's love in, they emerged as new women. This is God's version of an extreme makeover.

The guidebook offers a plan to help you deal with those old words, thoughts, and memories that threaten to plunge you into quicksand. But for now, consider this letter by another woman who lived through an ugly mess in her marriage and emerged reborn on the other side. May her story remind you that you are not alone, no matter what the Enemy of your soul wants to sell you to keep you in bondage and isolation.

ALLISON

It would be safe to say that I believed life couldn't get any better. I was married to my high-school sweetheart. We met at the church I grew up in. I believed I was married to Prince Charming. I adored him and believed in his fidelity to me. We had two beautiful gifts from God—our children: a daughter, thirteen, and our son, ten. We had family that we cherished, and they cherished us. We had a wonderful church where we celebrated God's presence in our lives. We had a terrific group of Christian friends. We enjoyed a beautiful home with an exceptional yard for entertaining. We worked hard and played hard. We created great memories through togetherness at home and on holidays and through frequent vacations. We counted all these as blessings from God.

On the eve of my fifteenth wedding anniversary, my kingdom came crashing down around me. My nightmare began as I learned that my husband was addicted to pornography. His path of sexual infidelity in mind, body, and soul caused devastation in my heart and soul in the days, months, and year to follow.

With this betrayal of our vows, of trust and intimacy, I didn't have the desire or strength to live but for my precious children. The prayers and heartache shared with those most dear strengthened my ability to go on. The hope of healing and restoration was a road I wasn't familiar with. I'm continuing to seek God's navigation on this journey.

Tomorrow is our nineteenth wedding anniversary. From the beginning of this unintended journey, my husband sought healing and restoration. Then he took his eyes off the prize, his downward spiral opened the gates to hell, and we entered once again. In that season I chose to focus on the power of addiction. I clung to hopelessness and fear. I now know that fear and faith cannot coexist. I've tried to make them marriage partners but realize that failure is the result. I know that fear had to be overcome by faith in God's supreme power and sovereignty. I'm grateful and blessed that my husband has returned and stayed on his path of purity. I'm grateful and blessed to have obeyed God's call to watch and wait; to depend only on Him to do the mighty work required; to grow strong and confident in who I am in Christ. I'm grateful and blessed for God's protection of my precious children. I'm grateful and blessed for the renewal and restoration of my marriage, as we share new respect, communication, support, tenderness, and passion beyond my highest expectations.

Is this going to be a happily-ever-after story? Without a doubt. Happily ever after with my King, my Lord, my Savior, my Knight in shining armor! I've craved to feel beautiful and complete. I've not always searched in the right places. I've struggled with destructive thoughts, depression, panic attacks, feelings of worthlessness and futility. I've turned to alcohol to numb my heartache. My life is not a fairy tale.

But now I've learned to love myself as Christ loves me, beautiful and complete. I will never leave His presence. He is precious to me, and I to Him. He alone is worthy of my trust. He alone is faithful and true.

> It is better to trust the Lord than to put confidence in men.
> It is better to take refuge in him than in the mightiest king!
> (Psalm 118:8–9, TLB)

12

The View Through Hefner's Eyes

Many men walk into marriage with a skewed perspective of intimacy. From the time of boyhood, men are exposed to ideas and situations that set them on a path to dysfunction in their most intimate relationships. Fifty years ago, many boys' first introduction to sexuality came from photos in *Playboy.* Prior to that, there was less graphic and less available material, but it was obtainable for the determined, nonetheless.

In our current culture, just a click of the computer's mouse can expose the curious boy to images that make *Playboy* look tame. No average female or simple bedroom sex can begin to compare to the images before him and to where his imagination has taken him. An adolescent boy, shy around real girls, feels awkward in his attempts to have meaningful female friendships and fears girls' rejection. He finds a pretense of comfort, love, and excitement in a fictional world of perfect female images. He can create a fantasy relationship where there is no risk of rejection. She has no personal needs, but she knows exactly what he needs emotionally and physically and fulfills those needs in his imaginary world. A young man will masturbate and bond to these images in his head; in doing so, he taps into a euphoric physical chemistry that was meant to be reserved as a gift to be shared in the union of marriage.

Here is a quote from Hugh Hefner, the founder of *Playboy,* on the state of the union:

> We all now live, to some extent, in a *Playboy* world. I can see
> the effects of the magazine and its campaign for sexual openness
> everywhere. I won! It's nice to have gone through the battles with
> all those Puritans, all the forces of repression and hypocrisy, and
> live long enough to see the victory parade.

I have to agree with him that he has won many battles, but the war isn't over. His victory, though, is every man's defeat. In all male settings where Clay speaks, a *minimum* of 80 percent of men will acknowledge having difficulty with or outright enslavement to pornographic images. These men aren't experiencing any so-called freedom that Mr. Hefner speaks of.

I want to clarify a point here. The definition of pornography is simply "the depiction of an image intended to arouse sexual desire." A man does not need to see a naked woman in order to be aroused sexually. Alluring dialogue, provocative clothing, seductive gestures, suggestive behavior—all have the power to elicit sexual desire. With that definition in mind, many of our current television commercials qualify, including ads for everything from breath mints to skin lotions. Victoria's *real* secret is that the company has put in-your-face pornography in shopping-mall windows, unsolicited catalogues, commercials, and annually televised "fashion shows." The average woman has been made to feel silly and insecure when she voices her discomfort as her husband gawks at these erotic parades. Many parents consider MTV standard teen fare, yet much of the video content and the commercials would have been rated X by the movie industry a few decades ago. Do you see why Mr. Hefner is so pleased? Porn has so infiltrated our culture, has become so acceptable, that the whole family views hours of pornographically saturated television every week.

Some boys may have had other destructive experiences, such as being befriended and then sexualized by an older boy or adult male. A boy who desperately needs a father figure in his life is a prime target for this exposure. That early conditioning may create confusion about sexuality.

Most men who have deep struggles with sexual integrity, including those who would describe themselves as heterosexual, say that they did not have a healthy relationship with their father. The lack of a loving, involved father in a boy's life weighs very heavily on the boy's becoming sexually obsessed later. Even if a father is present in the home, if he does not invest time with his son—spending quality and quantity time with him—and engage in activities with him, and teach him about the powerful influence of his sexual urges, the father leaves a gaping void in his son's life.

IT'S STILL A MATTER OF CHOICE

All that said, a boy may come from a healthy family with loving, connected parents and still make unhealthy choices. A wholesome upbringing does not guarantee flawless children. None of us is perfect, and we have to remind ourselves that God gave each of us free will.

Single men who have given themselves permission to satisfy their urges and are already in the habit of using substitutes are often of the false belief that they will no longer be interested in these activities once they are married. They believe that having the availability of a sexual partner 24/7 will give them the outlet they desire for sexual activity. What they don't take into account is that they have conditioned their minds for a specific type of stimuli; these extramarital sexual activities don't require anything of them in the forging and nurturing of a relationship. *Lovemaking* with a marriage partner is about *giving* to your spouse. The sexual activities the man has become accustomed to are all about *taking* for self-gratification.

I think of men's sexuality as their Achilles heel. Male sexuality is a powerful force, but when a boy or man does not guard his sexuality by exercising restraint in his thought life, his undisciplined mind and eyes often lead to compromised behavior. Exercising wisdom and protecting his sexuality give a man power. He becomes more productive, more creative, and more prosperous. He grows more loving and connected to his wife and children.

On the other hand, a man who lives life unleashed from any constraints eventually becomes powerless, with no self-control. He may think that his sexual behavior does not affect other areas of his life, but that belief is false. A study completed back in 1940 gives us a big-picture view of how sexuality affects our lives.

THE UNWIN REPORT

J. D. Unwin, a British social anthropologist, spent seven years studying the births and deaths of eighty-six civilizations spanning more than five thousand years. In *Hopousia* or *The Sexual and Economic Foundations of a New Society* (New York: Piest, 1940, page 82), he reported from his exhaustive research that *every* known culture in the world's history has followed the same sexual pattern.

During their early development, societies promoted sexual purity and prohibited sexual immorality, defined as premarital and extramarital sexual relationships. Great creative energy, associated with this inhibition of sexual expression, caused individuals, families, and the culture to prosper. By the societies' midlives, people began to rebel against sexual-purity prohibitions, demanding the freedom to express their internal passions. As values weakened, the social energy abated with increased indebtedness for individuals, families, and society. Finally, as the society became fully mature, people scoffed at sexual purity and freely expressed their lack of sexual inhibitions, which eventually resulted in loss of creative energy and the decay and destruction of the civilization.

Unwin concluded that the energy that holds a society together is sexual in nature. When a man is devoted to one woman and one family, he is motivated to build, save, protect, plan, and prosper on their behalf. However, when male and female sexual interests are dispersed and generalized, men invest their efforts in the gratification of sensual desires.

Unwin further noted: "Any human society is free either to display great energy, or to enjoy sexual freedom; the evidence is that they cannot do both for more than one generation."

The actual results of living by self-proclaimed, so-called freedoms do not ultimately give us freedom at all, but rather deplete every aspect of our lives. Based on Unwin's study, we are living in a civilization right now that has progressed into the mature stage of sexual freedoms.

AN UNPROTECTED WORLD

The word sex is the most used search word on the Internet. Our home computers give us all access to the most provocative and vilest sexual images imaginable. There is a full-fledged effort to redefine the definition of marriage, and at the same time, marriage is becoming less relevant to those for whom it was originally intended.

Our world mocks those individuals intent on preserving their virginity until marriage as repressed and unsophisticated. Unwanted pregnancy, just one result of sex "without consequences," has resulted in thirty-five million recorded abortions in the United States since abortion was legalized in 1973. AIDS began as a sexually transmitted disease, and the majority of people who become HIV positive are still infected in this manner. Vast numbers are innocent victims of this disease, yet there is almost a total absence of accountability among those who continue to spread the disease.

We expect teens to be teachable and persuaded to exercise self-control in all areas of life—academics, sports, smoking, alcohol, drugs, driving, eating habits—with one exception: sex. So instead of a truly comprehensive education on sexuality, which includes explaining the responsibility, risks, and consequences that accompany the freedom, and instead of teaching teens how to avoid temptation, our public schools simply equip them to do it with lowered risk.

Unprotected (New York: Sentinel, 2006) is a revealing book by an anonymous staff psychiatrist at UCLA (later disclosed to be Miriam Grossman, MD). It echoes my deep concerns. In her role with the university, the author exposes the pressure she faced to give students the politically correct line or risk censure and possible firing. She says campus health workers can ask about everything to do with students' physical conditions, but never about sexual matters. The practice results in blatant hypocrisy. A student can be forced to be tested for TB, but gay male students who have unprotected sex with countless partners are free to choose not to have an HIV test. Overall, the author says, there is a predominant attitude among those counseling students on their health that the sex drive is the strongest force on the planet. It's as though no healthy young person could resist the power of surging hormones, even though allowing this attitude to go unchecked can have dire health consequences. In 1960, there were only two sexually transmitted infections that were big concerns; now the number is more like twenty-five. And the prevailing attitude among campus health counselors is that each is perfectly common and normal.

The evidence in *Unprotected* is overwhelming: the very health professionals students look to for advice are steering them toward behaviors that are known to harm while belittling those that can actually help.

Even if the Bible were your only historical reference, it is obvious that there is nothing new when it comes to sexual indiscretion. Its pages are replete with stories of individuals and entire cultures that gave in to so-called sexual freedom. In the Old Testament, God, in His anger, wiped out entire civilizations for this very reason. Chapters 2 through 9 of Proverbs are almost entirely devoted to warning men to be on guard against the danger and destruction that await those who fall prey to improper sexual temptation.

> Listen to me, my son! I know what I am saying; listen!... For
> the lips of a prostitute are as sweet as honey, and smooth flattery
> is her stock in trade. But afterwards only a bitter conscience is
> left to you, sharp as a double-edged sword. She leads you down
> to death and hell. For she does not know the path to life.
> (Proverbs 5:1, 3–6, TLB)

In our companion guidebook, I devote an entire chapter to the immediate and long-term effects of pornography on male sexuality. But the good news? It doesn't have to be like this. For men willing to put God first and do the work of becoming disciplined in their sexuality, there is hope for a changed mind, changed heart, and changed behavior. There is hope for every individual, every marriage. As my husband, Clay, knows, true freedom is possible. Listen as he recounts his experience.

CLAY'S STORY

At the depths of my addiction, I was acting out every day. It was never enough. I always wanted and sought out more. Regardless of the frequency, I wasn't able to experience what my heart really desired—true intimacy, acceptance, love, joy, and peace. I was experiencing sheer agony, because what my heart really desired became more elusive as I sank ever deeper in my addiction.

Who would have thought that while I was "at the bottom," the Holy Spirit would want to have a conversation with *me*? Yet it happened. The conversation was brief but powerful. As I was acting out and rationalizing my actions, thinking things like, *I deserve it, I need it for stress relief, I'm only hurting myself,* the Holy Spirit told me my actions *changed things.* I asked, *What things does it change?* It wasn't until I worked through the countless layers of recovery that I came to understand the Holy Spirit's one-word answer: *Everything.* I came to find out that *everything* doesn't leave *anything* out!

My compromised behavior changed everything in my life, negatively impacting my marriage, my career, my finances, my friendships, my relationship with God, and on and on. Then during my recovery process, the Holy Spirit spoke to me through a teaching. He said if I wanted to change, I would have to give Him my whole heart, holding nothing back. I felt a pull of resistance, and I wrestled with Him. I asked what He would do with my whole heart, and He replied, *I will give you a new heart. I will change everything.*

> Then it will be as though I had sprinkled clean water on you, for you will be clean—your filthiness will be washed away, your idol worship gone. And I will give you a new heart—I will give you new and right desires—and put a new spirit within you. I will take out your stony hearts of sin and give you new hearts of love. (Ezekiel 36:25–26, TLB)

13

I Want My Life Back

M aybe your response to all you've read so far is: *Just tell me how
to get my husband to stop his behavior now.* You want everything
to return to normal. If there were a book on the shelf titled *How to Fix
Your Husband in Three Easy Steps,* you probably would have passed on
this one and walked away with that one.

I wish I could tell you there is a magical 1-2-3 formula. Unfortunately, there isn't, but be assured that the guidebook devotes numerous
sections to helping you be most effective in motivating your husband to
become a new man. We also will help you differentiate between what
you can influence and what you can't. The Avenue ministry guidebook
series for men is the prescription for a man with sexual integrity issues.
My prayer is that the husband of every woman reading this book is also
willing to reach out for the help available, by joining and completing an
Avenue men's group healing study.

Maybe your perspective is, *If he doesn't have a problem, then I don't
have a problem.* While I can't offer an ironclad guarantee that your husband is going to get with the program, I hope it will encourage you that

many men do, with the appropriate prompting by their wives. I can guarantee you, though, that even if you could wave a wand that would change him overnight, you would undoubtedly still be left holding a bag of unwelcome debris that contains some weighty or toxic substances: anger, grief, bitterness, jealousy, or worse. You might also be dwelling on getting revenge or payback for his betrayals. Maybe you are tormented, replaying your husband's behavior in your mind.

You wouldn't be human if you didn't experience some intense emotions right now; they are all natural feelings when you've been betrayed by someone you trusted. You may even be incapacitated by depression or engulfed in self-loathing. Those things don't magically disappear just because he gets his act together. In fact, sometimes they escalate. Maybe now he's doing great, and in contrast you may feel like you've been passed by, lying wounded on the side of the road. So unless you've got that same magic formula handy to do a number on yourself, expect that there will be collateral damage to heal from.

Still, you need to know your husband is not the person who can fix all this for you. Your husband will need to take ownership of many things. Being worthy of trust again is up to him. Putting healthy boundaries in place to guard his sexual integrity is his responsibility. But he doesn't have the power to repair your soul; only you can make that choice. Only you can take the steps needed to move forward, one foot in front of the other, to come to a new, healthy place. Unless you address those feelings, you will suffer, and your marriage will ultimately suffer from the wounds that were denied or unattended to.

Regardless of your personal history and that of your partner, it's most likely that nothing in your life to date has prepared you fully to deal with the place you are in now. Each woman on an unintended journey finds herself in a foreign place with a new set of issues. Each woman has hurts, concerns, and decisions to make. But you will have to process through that mixed bag of emotions for your own healing.

A New Perspective

No matter to what extent your relationship has been assaulted or whether or not your relationship with this man survives the storm, you will come to view some aspects of both life and marriage from a new perspective. Many changes you may make will be welcome ones, even if the way they first came about is not. To a great extent, this struggle is what will compel you to change. Wherever you end up, from now on things will be different; *you will be different.* Becoming different than you were can be either positive or negative. The good news is that you have the ability to influence how you change through the way you respond, either with fear or with hope.

Hopefully, you will find the key to guarding your heart, and it will not turn to stone. Hopefully, you will be less naive about the risk you take when you make yourself vulnerable in your relationship again. Hopefully, you will become more authentic in all your relationships. Hopefully, you will encourage your husband to be his authentic self in your presence. Hopefully, you will develop a whole new depth of intimacy with your husband. Hopefully, you will take better care of your emotional, spiritual, and physical self. Hopefully, you will become more compassionate, encouraging, and forgiving of others. Hopefully, you will find yourself understanding Jesus a little better.

Even with the possibility that you will become a better you through this trial, you might also adopt new perspectives that will produce a changed but less wonderful you. If you remain mindful that you always have that choice, hopefully you won't make poor decisions based on fear or numb your true feelings, and you will not become bitter or callous. You will not pull away from valuable relationships or let this difficulty define the rest of your life. You won't settle for the mediocre or hide in shame. You won't become skeptical or distrustful of men. You won't become judgmental or unforgiving, punishing yourself or putting on blinders to avoid the truth. Hopefully, you won't decide to stop loving.

Yet if only you had a magic wand, all of this would be so much easier. Magic wands of fairy tales are simply make believe, but God gives us real *power tools* to transform our lives, to turn pain into joy, hatred into love, desolation into beauty. The same tools have the power to transform your husband's life as well, from deception into integrity, hardheartedness into tender-heartedness, failure into victory.

The power tools are contained in a very thick instruction manual. I know that many of us just want to use the tool and get to work; we'll read the manual if all else fails. But these tools cannot be accessed without reading and following the instructions. These power tools I'm describing are contained in the Bible. Using the Bible's instructions will open up pathways to change and freedom that were possibly unknown to you before. But they also have limits. Unlike the wands of fairy tales, God's power tools do not impose themselves on us, but allow free will.

Maybe you already own several Bibles and can even recite some favorite parts. Now you are in a new situation, and the instructions will take on fresh meaning. That I guarantee. Finding your way through comes not from discovering a *new* revelation, but from learning and understanding an *old* one on a deeper level. The rock-solid boulders of wisdom are not recent discoveries but time-tested truths that have held their ground against the forces of age and erosion. It can't be overstressed that reading the truth is one thing, and doing it is another. The truth doesn't improve our lives until we internalize what we read, listen to God speaking, and take action.

> We have not been telling you fairy tales when we explained to
> you the power of our Lord Jesus Christ and his coming again.
> My own eyes have seen his splendor and his glory....

So we have seen and proved that what the prophets said
came true. You will do well to pay close attention to everything
they have written, for, like lights shining into dark corners, their
words help us to understand many things that otherwise would
be dark and difficult. But when you consider the wonderful
truth of the prophets' words, then the light will dawn in your
souls and Christ the Morning Star will shine in your hearts.
(2 Peter 1:16, 19, TLB)

Some women say they don't get anything out of reading the Bible.
None of it seems pertinent to their circumstance. And while the Bible
needs nothing added to it, a guide can help direct you to specific areas
for your immediate needs. As this proverb highlights, effectively delivering wisdom also requires good timing.

Everyone enjoys giving good advice, and how wonderful
it is to be able to say the right thing at the right time!
(Proverbs 15:23, TLB)

We've intended the guidebook to offer that kind of well-timed
guidance. There we point you to specific sections of the Bible that will
be pertinent to your present needs.

But what are these power tools? Simply, God's principles for a
peace-filled life. *Wisdom* to know how to make the right choices. *Prayer*
as a direct conduit to talk to God and hear from Him. The *Holy Spirit*
to guide and encourage us. *Armor* and *weapons* to protect us from the
snare of the Enemy.

The guidebook might be seen as a jumpstart to accessing the tools,
but there is so much more in the Bible to discover that will strengthen
your journey. I believe that through this circumstance the Bible could
become a valuable companion for the rest of your life.

Angry Women with Hammers
Should Be Avoided

Consider this story of a woman who knew the Bible well. Unfortunately, she used what she read not as a tool to improve her life or the lives of those around her but instead as a blunt weapon.

Alex and Ellie had been married for six years and had two young children when Alex confessed to her that he had been unfaithful. He was weighed down by guilt and didn't want to repeat his failure. Naturally, Ellie didn't receive the news with much grace. Alex didn't know what to do other than offer his apology and promise never to let it happen again. Ellie didn't know how to deal with the anger she felt, and her initial righteous anger became an arrogant stance of unforgiving anger.

She said she forgave him, but she knew well what the Bible said about infidelity, and she used that to assault Alex at every opportunity, month after month and year after year. Ellie didn't often speak directly of the betrayal, but its shadow clouded every interaction they had.

Although Ellie attended Mass every day, she walked out the same person she walked in. Alex was by nature a quiet, soft-spoken man, and as Ellie grew more bitter by the year, Alex became even quieter. Although years passed, the sting of the betrayal was as fresh as the day of confession for Ellie. Through the years, that sting became laced with disdain, resentment, and disrespect for Alex as a man. Alex was walled up in a prison of shame, hammered down by Ellie's critical tongue. Even in a roomful of people, he disappeared into the wallpaper.

Ellie's criticism began to affect every area of her life. As she grew older, even her grandchildren were afraid around her because of her condescending tone. Alex finally found peace in death at age fifty-nine, although he appeared much older. Ellie lived another thirty years as the bitter woman everyone tried to avoid.

This may sound extreme, but Ellie is not that unusual. I have met many a woman who came to despise the man she called her husband. Many had the "till death do us part" vow nailed, but they never took steps to create peace in their own hearts or renew love for their husbands. They allowed hurt, anger, or depression to dictate how they lived. Will you, by default, allow your unresolved hurt and unforgiveness to rule the rest of your life? Or will you take the steps needed to be the author of your emotional health and get your life back?

No Package Deals

Let's consider another situation. You have already made the decision to leave him, or he has left you; the decision to divorce has been made. Wouldn't it be a great package deal if we could divorce the hurt and hatred at the same time we leave the marriage? I have learned from personal experience that divorce is not an all-inclusive, final deal. In legal terms, divorce has finality, but in the emotional, spiritual, and physical realms, it has no end. You can't divorce your emotions. You may wrestle with your religious belief on the issue; you'll probably have a new financial status. You'll face practical and emotional issues involving some or all of the following: children, in-laws, mutual friends, and your ex and his new mate. These issues may have to be navigated for the rest of your life. If you desire to build a new life after divorce on a foundation of emotional, physical, and spiritual health, you will have a healing process to journey through.

Betsy is one woman who walked in those very shoes and journeyed through to a better place. Listen to what she says.

Betsy

I had been married about ten years when I found out that my husband had had multiple affairs. He traveled a lot on business and had a lot of unaccountable time. When I discovered the truth, I totally cratered. I felt completely alone. It was a very difficult time, not knowing which end was up, feeling numb inside. I felt like I was the only one in the world going through these things. I remember one day at work, sitting at my desk and wondering if anyone realized I had been there all day doing nothing. I couldn't function. I couldn't even lift a pen.

The day my husband left to live in another state, I found out about Avenue ministries. I went to my first women's retreat, where Susan Allen shared her story. I was flabbergasted that any woman, especially in the church, had gone through what I was going through and knew the pain and the depth of emotion I was feeling. Yet she had found her way through, and she knew how to get there. I couldn't believe it. I made up my mind right there that I was going to find out about the ministry and get help for myself.

I went to the Unintended Journey study, which provided the support and direction to help me through a three-year separation. That separation ended when my husband returned, thinking maybe he would like to be married after all. Though we had been married for ten years, it was a nonmarriage for the majority of those years. We came back together, and nothing in him had really changed. But I was a different person. God had strengthened me from the inside out. Going through Unintended Journey, I learned that somewhere along the way I lost myself during my marriage. God had me start from the bottom, clearing out the rubble of everything that had caved in. What He showed me was, *This is who you are; this is who I made you to be; this is where I want you to start over, regardless of what your husband chooses.*

My husband ended up leaving again, and we divorced. But the difference this time was that I didn't crater. God had shown me how to be strong and how to be the woman He created me to be. My husband had lived a secret life for years, and I had lived in a lot of denial during those years, but I finally realized that denial is not the way to go. In my life God said, *Even if your marriage doesn't survive* (and it didn't), *you are strong, you are beautiful, and you are My creation.*

I want to tell the women reading this right now who don't know if their marriages are going to survive or not: even if your marriage doesn't survive, it's not so much about the end, but about the process. He wants to take you through to healing, regardless of the outcome. It's about the process of finding out who you are and who God made you to be and of truly knowing that God is on your side.

You cannot control the actions and the decisions of your husband, and there may be some of you who are already in a divorce situation and feeling totally lost, totally hopeless. Yet even though it's not God's desire that marriages dissolve, it's not your fault. What I can tell you, now that I've been divorced for several years, is that *God is good.* But to come to a better place, I had to put my energy and heart into following God. Even though He is still working on a lot of pieces inside me, I'm okay. Even though my marriage didn't survive, I did. Let me offer you encouragement and hope; by taking this journey, you will discover your way, your true beauty, and that God loves you very much.

And He will be with you every step of the way.

I have spoken to many women about their perspectives on this unintended journey they've been thrust into. Those who feel they have received insight from God about this circumstance essentially arrive at three different conclusions.

First, some women conclude that they married for all the right reasons, that both of them were living Christ-centered lives, and that somewhere along the way their husbands made a wrong decision. Other women know without a doubt that God brought them together to marry, and they came to understand later that He wanted their marriages to be a conduit to help them work through old issues in their lives. The third conclusion some women come to is that God warned them in advance about their husbands' characters, but they put on blinders or believed they would fix the men or went forward anyway because of their own longings.

In these situations, different circumstances brought the couples together, but one thing is consistent. Once couples marry, God blesses the union and doesn't want it to fall apart. His hope is that with husband and wife "becoming as one," the sinful nature of each person will be challenged and encouraged to change by the love and limits of the other. Every spouse invariably ends up having to face his or her own failings. Within God's perfect plan, the two will draw closer to God through every challenge, and the marriage itself will become a more accurate reflection of our relationship with God.

The linchpin in that last sentence is "within God's perfect plan." Many couples don't work out their failings together to become better people and partners. One spouse continues in destructive sin, or the other person hardens her heart regardless of her spouse's repentance. That's free will at work. God has laid out for us how He would have us respond to the failings of our spouses, but we always have a choice. And our spouses have the choice of whether to continue in destructive sin or end it.

I've found that it's the women who choose to trust in God's perfect plan for their lives and marriages who realize the greatest rewards, like Betsy did, despite the final outcome.

14

Journey to a Better Place

The process of healing the heart involves traveling a well-marked path. Many people simply hope for healing of their emotions and have no understanding of the definitive measures God gave us to assure a positive outcome. How God heals a wounded heart is a mystery, but it is not a gamble. Personal growth is a natural outcome of the healing process. Growth is enormous if it has been stunted while you were preoccupied with destructive forces or devastating loss. Just as the scripture below states, if you follow God's lead, healing is a certainty. Hear that again: it is a certainty.

> In everything you do, put God first, and he will direct you and crown your efforts with success. (Proverbs 3:6, TLB)

Dotted throughout the Scriptures are verses that speak of a path, a road, a street, or an avenue. Some paths are wide, some are narrow, some are stately, some are simple, some are paved, and some are not. In some verses God is encouraging us to follow a path He wants to guide us on. In others, He warns us of ones to avoid. He is your guide, walking ahead of you, protecting you and preparing the way.

> You are my hiding place from every storm of life; you even keep
> me from getting into trouble! You surround me with songs of
> victory. I will instruct you (says the Lord) and guide you along
> the best pathway for your life; I will advise you and watch your
> progress. (Psalm 32:7–8, TLB)

THIS UNINTENDED JOURNEY

Imagine your entire life as a journey. Each person is on a personal journey from the moment of birth to the point of departure from this world. Some paths branch off, and some intersect with others at crossroads. These paths represent the choices in your life. Some of the pathways you choose are lovely, wide, safe, and uncluttered. Yet at certain points, the paths change, the clearings around them narrow, and you can't see what lies ahead. Some paths you will have to travel are not what you'd choose.

Many stones are scattered along your path; some are pebbles, others are boulders. Each stone represents a circumstance, a person, or an event in your life. Some stones are beautiful, representing important persons, things of value, or cherished moments along your way. Others hinder your progress. You can't be aware of all of them, and you'll likely stub your toe on a few. Others you are acutely aware of, and you'll have to intentionally avoid them. Some are small enough to kick out of your way, and others you may simply walk on, minor discomforts that only slow you down a bit.

The Scriptures are bursting with analogies built upon stones. Stones are used to represent places, people, concepts, and even weapons. There are also some very special rocks that offer you protection and safety, as in this verse:

> The Lord is my fort where I can enter and be safe; no one can
> follow me in and slay me. He is a rugged mountain where I
> hide; he is my Savior, a rock where none can reach me, and a
> tower of safety. He is my shield. (Psalm 18:2, TLB)

Scripture offers dozens of references to God as our Rock of protection, a place of refuge. Because God is always present no matter where you are on your path, His rock—a shield and a fortress—is within your reach. Even though in your life you are experiencing an unwelcome change, God's character and His promises never change. He is always standing ready to provide shelter for you, whatever your circumstance.

The part of your journey you're currently traveling could be described as a narrow, rocky, and hilly path. It isn't a path you chose; your husband chose it. Now there you are. It's difficult to navigate and impossible to see ahead. In order to move forward, you must excavate an avalanche of rocks that completely block the trail.

The book in your hands is a tool to help you get your bearings. To move beyond this roadblock, help you navigate the right course to your personal healing, and evaluate the possibility of restoring your marriage, you will need the guidebook and your Bible. The guidebook is gleaned from my personal experiences, Bible studies, studies specific to this subject, and conversations with numerous women about their circumstances, all while overseeing eleven years of small groups for women on this journey. Of course, each woman's journey is slightly different. I am not on a mission for you to follow a prescribed program or lead you to a predetermined destination. What I hope is that the process will heighten your own awareness of God's voice to direct your footsteps.

> Show me the path where I should go, O Lord; point out the
> right road for me to walk. Lead me; teach me; for you are
> the God who gives me salvation. I have no hope except in
> you. (Psalm 25:4–5, TLB)

LANDMARKS

The guidebook provides landmarks, sort of like You Are Here cues on a map, to help you clearly recognize where you are in your journey. Each chapter in the guidebook acts as one of these landmarks, which have been erected by those who went before you. Some landmarks will direct you to stop and look at the stones dotting the path. The guidebook will help you identify each one for what it is, help you make sense of what you are facing, and give you encouragement to decide what to do with particular stones. Many stones need to be turned over to reveal what is hiding underneath. Sometimes it's not so pretty. Some stones are so heavy that we can't move them with our own strength. We need the help of others. Some stones that represent destructive forces need to be hurled out of our paths.

Regardless of the issues, many stones represent something that requires both introspection and action. Your current condition will determine what action you need to take before continuing on to the next stone. When you are faced with new realities or stones you haven't been able to face yet, you may need to spend a lot of time in introspection. There comes a point, though, when you need to take action to correct unhealthy conditions. Introspection without action can keep you walking in circles around a stone, obsessing about what may be under the stone and never moving on. On the other hand, if you pass by the landmarks and stones at breakneck speed and don't stop to ponder or take heed, you could be seriously hurt and even cause damage to others.

Some landmarks are placed at a fork in the road where you have to identify options and make wise decisions about which way to go. If you don't stop to think about your direction, you may travel a long distance in the wrong direction, bringing more harm to yourself, traipsing through places that are fruitless or even dangerous. Without willingness to receive godly guidance, you will have taken a long journey to come to a dead-end road more wounded and weary, needier and hungrier for help, than when you started.

> A prudent [woman] foresees the difficulties ahead and prepares for them; the simpleton goes blindly on and suffers the consequences. (Proverbs 22:3, TLB)

The many landmarks you'll encounter in the guidebook directly address these questions and more:

- *Are my emotions normal?*
- *Do I stay, divorce, or separate?*
- *How can I know if my husband is at it again?*
- *Do I react to my situation in unhealthy or destructive ways?*
- *Why does he keep breaking his promises?*
- *How can I create firm boundaries without becoming harsh?*
- *How can I distinguish between truth and a lie?*
- *How can love work when I've been so unloved?*
- *How can I know where my marriage and life will end up?*
- *How can I know if he is worthy of my trust again?*
- *Have I lost myself in my desperation to please my husband?*
- *Has my own past hindered having a healthy relationship?*
- *What does a faithful husband actually look like?*
- *How do I protect my children?*
- *Will I ever stop feeling this way?*

For every question, there is an answer, and in the guidebook you'll find solid information to help you draw your *own* conclusions. When your answer indicates that something is broken and needs fixing, we offer direction on the process to repair or rebuild. Hungry for insight, many women have read through the guidebook in a few days, finding a wealth of information relating to the very thing you are going through right now. Just as this book has helped you get your bearings, the guidebook will inundate you with specific help to keep you moving forward.

15

Who Are Your Hiking Buddies?

Any experienced hiker will tell you that you should never head out alone, especially if you are unfamiliar with the trail. We have all heard stories of people who went for a short hike and didn't return. Their only hope was that a team of people equipped to help would come looking for them and bring them back to safety.

I have learned one important lesson that I cannot overemphasize: having other women to share your difficulties will make all the difference in helping you make wise decisions and end up in a healthier place. Whether or not your marriage survives, what you need more than anything else is the fellowship of a few other women who will hold your hand, listen to you, encourage you with God's hope for your future, pray and walk with you. You will gain wisdom from the guidance of others who have already experienced this part of the journey.

Is there any such thing as Christians cheering each other up? Do you love me enough to want to help me? Does it mean anything

to you that we are [sisters] in the Lord, sharing the same Spirit?
Are your hearts tender and sympathetic at all? Then make me
truly happy by loving each other and agreeing wholeheartedly
with each other, working together with one heart and mind and
purpose. (Philippians 2:1–2, TLB)

The benefits of walking with other women as you heal are inex-
haustible. Other women will become a mirror for you. As you listen to
their stories, you will see your own situation with more objectivity. You
will find a broader perspective of the common issues. You will experience
a healthy bond and friendship. Like women who have gone through
childbirth together or shared the sorrow of not being able to conceive,
you will experience a supportive relationship few others can match.

One incredible discovery that women always make in these groups
is the similarity of the lies they have been told. Even the ones they've
told themselves tend to be very common. The lie most women have in
common?

I am the reason for his behavior.

The women in a group may range from a twenty-year-old newly-
wed to a sixty-year-old grandmother and include every age, personality,
and body type in between. Yet to some degree, most have accepted some
responsibility for their husbands' failures. As each woman's isolation
begins to erode, she begins to see, often for the first time, that his behavior is not the result of a defect in her but a symptom of his own issues.

We hear varied statistics depending on the source, but *minimally*
30 percent of all marriages fall victim to infidelity at some point. And
more than 50 percent of men view pornography with varying degrees
of regularity. With those figures, the simple math concludes that in any
setting of women, about one third are going through what you are facing right now. Hear that again: one third of *all* married women. They
may not be wearing the evidence on the outside, but if they have uncov-

ered a husband's betrayal, they are just as anxious and uncertain about their day-to-day existence as you.

Isolation is the enemy of healing. It is our shame that keeps us silent. Our embarrassment about our situation keeps us locked up in secrets. We wear a mask to hide, often even with our best friends and family members. Maybe you attend church and look around at all the people, thinking their lives are as put together as their clean and pressed Sunday clothes. You feel like a fraud, thinking that if people were able to see into your life right now, they would be appalled and run.

BETH

One night the Lord woke me up. I felt like I was supposed to see why my husband was up so late.

I was so anxious walking toward his office. The door was only open a crack, just enough for me to see him sitting at the computer, nervously looking back and forth from the screen to the door. My heart pounded. I wasn't sure what was on the screen. I didn't want to believe it. But it was obvious. I felt anger well up inside me, and the next moment I was out of control, screaming at him and hitting him. I told him to call Clay right then or leave. A few years prior to this, he had gone through the program for the same problem and had a healing, or so I thought. I was in denial at that time, I guess. I didn't want to talk about it or my feelings at all. My husband was on his own.

He didn't call Clay that night, and he chose to leave. While he was gone, I read his workbook. *Wow.* I got so much insight. I didn't understand what sexual compulsivity was. I thought it was my fault my husband was acting out. He had always blamed me for it, and through all those years, I didn't want to talk about it to anyone. I didn't even want him to talk about it with me. I had been cloaked in shame that kept me from learning how to deal with the issues.

But now I knew the truth, and I wasn't about to let him pin the blame on me. He was back in the meetings that weekend and has since gone through the whole program again. Today he attends as a leader. He had a repentant heart from the beginning, so it was easy for me to forgive him. He no longer blames me for his issue, and we talk about his triggers.

This time I got into the women's group. There I found women who were not giving advice but speaking the truth about their own circumstances. It was a place where women could speak about their pain, where people understand and are sympathetic. I also found it to be a place where I could talk about victories and healing. At first I didn't want to share how God was moving in our marriage. I almost felt guilty for saying what a great husband I have. Then one night I said, "Do you think I'm wrong for trusting my husband?" That's when I realized what godly women these were. They encouraged me and rejoiced with me. They were all genuinely happy for the healing of my marriage, regardless of their individual circumstances. I can't tell you how good that felt, to know that these women were truly excited with me for what God had done. I thank God for the ministry of Avenue.

***

Beth is referring to the confidential small groups that Avenue helps to establish around the country. They provide a place for both men and women to meet to encourage one another through a difficult season. Beth found strength in the company of other women who knew exactly what she was dealing with. Getting support for herself not only helped her to let go of her shame but also increased her husband's likelihood of recovery, as well as the likelihood that their marriage would be restored.

Your husband's behavior may be so humiliating that you feel no one could understand. Living in quiet desperation and isolation, you may have allowed destructive things to happen to your own children because of your fears. But there is nothing new; anything that is happening in your world is happening in neighbors' homes not far from where you live. That may shock some, but I hope you recognize how much we all have in common. Regardless of our partner's actions, the feelings we experience are common. If we truly understood the nature of the issue, the scope of this pandemic, we would see how important it is to be allies in our mutual need.

So remember, there are women all around you wading in the same murky waters. What if you could confidentially connect with those women and find a safe place to be real about these struggles? Think about it.

A COMMUNITY OF WOMEN

Avenue paves the way, offering sound biblical guidance, hope, and tools to change your circumstances and find lasting healing. Avenue was conceived to create intimate and safe environments throughout the country for people with these common issues. For nearly a decade, Avenue has been helping churches, counselors, and individuals to offer these safe havens to those in need.

Sophie had been trying for many years to follow what she thought was the Christlike way to deal with her husband's failures. But she had limited information. She had a biblical concept about forgiveness, but it was incomplete.

SOPHIE

When I entered the Avenue class, I walked in with the idea that I needed to "forgive, forget, and never look back" on my husband's betrayals. After doing this two other times in our twenty-two-year relationship, I realized this wasn't the answer, but I didn't know what else to do. Through the material covered in the guidebook and my leader's counsel, I began to understand that not trusting didn't mean I hadn't forgiven him. This freed me tremendously and gave me a sense of empowerment over my situation. While my heart was freed from holding a grudge, I could still have my eyes wide open and take my time about whether to ever trust my husband again.

❋

Sophie needed to learn to draw boundaries on her unrepentant husband. For Sophie, it was a foreign idea that a person could forgive but not reconcile the relationship. She had dealt with her past betrayals in isolation, denying herself access to the insights of others who could offer true healing.

Many women who might avoid a small group altogether, or enter with guardedness and skepticism, are completely surprised at the sense of community, friendship, and intimacy these groups create. I know because I was one of those skeptics. I recall a time when I was fairly new to church. I was at a women's luncheon, and the speaker said we were going to break up into small groups to discuss a topic with the women seated at the table with us. I didn't stick around. I excused myself to go to the restroom and made a hasty exit to my car.

Of course, there's always a risk that your truth will not be well received, even by friends and family. Avenue's Unintended Journey groups are designed to protect your dignity and dispel your fears. These groups aren't composed of randomly selected women. Through reading this book, each woman has identified issues in her marriage that are on target with the problems we've described here. *Every woman* at an Avenue group table is on *this* unintended journey. Here is one woman's perspective on the value of going through the study with other women in the same situation.

EVE

The *moment* I heard about this group, I knew I needed that support. I am a drug and alcohol counselor who works with street women with addictions, so I am very aware of the miracles a body of people oriented toward God as their power can bring. I had no preconceived notions of what it would be like. I just knew that I needed to be in a group with God as the healer. The single best thing was that I wasn't alone. I had a place where I could honestly share what was going on with me. It was important for my healing.

The other women were all much younger than I, and I could see how I had been earlier in my marriage, thinking my husband's infidelity had everything to do with me and that there was something I could do to have him change. With my husband's latest infidelity (he was fifty-nine and I was fifty-seven), I knew it had nothing to do with me, except that I had tolerated it and taken responsibility for it. As I listened to the younger women and their tolerating behaviors, how they hoped prayer alone would alter their husbands, I realized that these women's reactions mirrored mine earlier in my marriage. It was really valuable for me to see why it took me so long to deal with this in a constructive way, how the situation can continue to persist when we passively live in false hope rather than seeing the truth clearly and taking action to protect ourselves.

The fellowship within my group became all the more precious when I experienced a painful loss of intimacy with my former friends. When I let my close friends know that Joe and I were in recovery, none of them wanted to talk about it. But in the Unintended Journey group, I could share this part of my life with these close friends and bear witness of our healing for God's glory.

God used my unintended journey to heal me in areas I had given up on having healed—in my life, in my husband's, and in our family. I can't imagine what would have occurred in our lives if Avenue had not been there.

Having facilitated other women's recovery groups, Eve knew firsthand the benefits of recovering with others. She was a "doctor needing the help of another doctor," and she didn't allow her experience or pride to stand in the way of getting specialized medicine for her unique circumstance.

Here are the words of a few other women sharing their group experiences. Their answers reflect the collective sentiments of the women I have heard from through the years.

What was your first reaction to the idea of being in such a group of women?

Corrine: My husband gave me a phone number to call for women's support, because he was in the Avenue men's group. But I felt so hurt and angry, thinking, *Why should I call to get help when it's his problem? He's the one who needs help.* I just wanted a quick fix for him and to forget it ever happened.

Pamela: I was very apprehensive, but I was also desperate. My friends felt inadequate to help me. So I called the Avenue phone-contact woman; she was so gracious and helpful! It was my lifeline!

Debbie: I knew I needed some help but had no clue how much I would gain by being in a group. I sought out Avenue at the suggestion of a friend. I'm a little ashamed to admit it, but at the time I believed I had more to contribute to help other women and didn't expect much help from them. I had no clue how much richness they would add to my life.

Kellie: After my first group meeting, all I felt was relief. I needed to be with these women who shared my values even though I didn't know them that well. I was eager and had thousands of questions swirling around my mind.

How did the group experience compare with your preconceived notion?

Corrine: I met a wonderful young mother of three small children, much like myself, who was going through the same thing. I had the chance to share with other women and pray with them, and they were there for me to call anytime of the day. Without that, I don't know how I would have climbed out of my depression.

Pamela: It was close to what I thought, though there was less structure for discussion of the week's topic than I expected, and the leader allowed a lot of sharing. My eyes were opened to a whole world I didn't know about. Everyone's perspective, the variety of experiences and circumstances—I wanted someone to just tell me what I was supposed to do in this totally new situation, but I didn't get that. Instead, I received information and guidance. I realized that I needed to take the responsibility of walking with God; I needed to focus on hearing from Him for direction.

Debbie: The reality was very different from my preconceived ideas. When I first heard the ladies' stories, I really thought my situation was not as bad as theirs and that I was further in my recovery and healing than they were. How wrong I was! As time went on, I learned to focus on myself and my own issues. I realized how much I needed help and that my thinking was really skewed. I was full of pride and an over-inflated view of myself. I realized how much I needed these women and how their insights and experiences would help me to gain perspective on my own situation. Their growth helped propel me in my own growth. I eventually learned to forgive my husband after only six months. I never thought that would be possible. I know it was because of Avenue and being with other women who were sharing their experiences.

Kellie: I didn't expect to heal. I expected the group would be a safe place to share my life and my feelings. But I never thought of true healing and being able to understand my husband's pain at the time I joined.

What was the single best thing that you experienced from being in a group?

Corrine: I just had to show up. It was my hope. It was the only place that gave me an outlet.

Pamela: That I wasn't alone. I had a place where I could honestly share what was going on with me and that was for my healing.

Debbie: The safety of being myself, warts and all, and feeling loved and accepted anyway. Being real resulted in some rich and lasting friendships with some of the women in the group. This ended up being a very special time in my life, and I will never forget it.

Kellie: I didn't expect that one day I would be able to say that addiction had been a part of my life without feeling shame or condemnation from those around me. Another outcome was the gradual shedding of the feeling that his addiction would control my actions and feelings forever.

What was the most unexpected outcome of knowing women with a common issue?

Corrine: That I wasn't the only one in our church with this problem. We relieved each other of our shame we had carried when we were isolated.

Pamela: The very first thing that hit me was that these were great women. There was nothing wrong with them! They didn't make this happen to themselves, nor did they deserve this. That led me to contemplate that perhaps I didn't either.

Debbie: When I run into any woman from my group, we smile and embrace each other, and immediately have that "knowing" connection. We've been through a terrible ordeal together, and we made it. Our hearts are healed, and we're going on with our lives.

Kellie: Once I began hearing the pain in the voices of other women who had recently found out [about their husbands' betrayal], somehow it made my own pain less intense and bearable.

What negative things happened in the company of these women?

Corrine: I didn't experience anything negative in the group or in my contact with them between group meetings.

Pamela: Sometimes I would carry things home. I would suspect my husband of things that weren't true that had been exposed at the group. Since there was no honesty at our house, I was very suspicious of many things already.

Debbie: If a woman's story was similar to mine, I would feel anger toward her husband and her for allowing him to do whatever it was he was doing. But through the gracious and patient help of my facilitator, I soon realized that I was angry at my own husband and myself and that I needed to get honest about it. Through the group and the curriculum, I came to connect that, as a child, it had not been okay to be angry in my home. But when others were treated unjustly, this gave me an excuse for my anger to surface. It caused a lot of tension in the group for a few weeks. But as I began to see the truth, things got better. I had to apologize and ask for forgiveness from those I had offended.

Kellie: I can't say anything negative happened in the group.

Many hundreds of women have healed wounds and overcome obstacles in their lives with the groups as a catalyst. Some have restored their marriages. Others have found the strength to start over when their marriages imploded. Avenue groups are a vehicle to help you move forward toward the goal of restoration for your body, mind, and spirit. Freedom and new beginnings aren't just for the lucky few when you allow God to direct your path.

Each group meets two hours once a week for the six-month study. There is time to discuss the weekly topic in the guidebook, voluntarily share your personal challenges and victories, and pray. Together with your hiking buddies, you can accelerate your dig through the rubble of sorrow-filled days. You can trek every step together to your destination of hearts filled with hope.

Remember, just like with Dorothy's yellow brick road, your journey was not your intention. Dorothy's world was turned upside down, and her only way to find home again was to walk into the unknown. But strengthened by new friends who hoped to find what they were looking for, she and her friends accomplished what they didn't have the fortitude to do individually.

16

Getting Started

There are several ways to put yourself in the company of other women dealing with these issues. One way is to join an existing group in your community. Go to our Web site, AvenueResource.com. Click on "Join a confidential Avenue group," and follow the instructions to find a group near you. You can also call our confidential, toll-free call center at 1-877-326-7000 to ask for the same information.

Another way is to create your own small group. There are several reasons you might want to start your own; for example, your immediate area has no group or the group doesn't meet at a time that works with your schedule. You can get your own group together in several ways, especially if you don't let the idea of being the initiator intimidate you. Read on, and you will find a model that fits you.

FINDING A FACILITATOR

Rather than putting your needs on hold because you don't have a group in your area, equip yourself to create your own small Avenue group.

Your group can be as small as two people: yourself and one other woman willing to meet. If you aren't sure who to ask, try these options:

- Do you know a woman affected by these issues in the past? Maybe a family member, a friend, or a co-worker would be willing to meet once a week to go through the guidebook with you.

- Ask your church to recommend a woman who would be willing to meet with you.

- A Christian counselor could go through the weekly curriculum with you. You can even expand upon her resources and ask if she would be willing to facilitate a group with other women she counsels with the same need.

OTHER OPTIONS

You might consider approaching your women's ministry leader. Print a page from our Web site to offer her, and ask her to consider the benefits of beginning an Avenue chapter for the community. The leadership can visit our Web site to learn more.

Alternatively, you may be able to facilitate a new group in your church. Some women going through this journey are able to facilitate groups, while others have too much stress to add this responsibility.

If you have already been through an Unintended Journey group, you may be the perfect candidate, even if you feel as though you still need more support yourself. As you read through the upcoming section on facilitating, consider this vital role to create continued healing for yourself and other women in your church and community.

If you are reading this book to understand and support a woman in this situation and/or have healed from your own unintended journey, the Unintended Journey leader's guide and curriculum will provide you with the resources and encouragement to be a place of refuge in her time of need. Oftentimes, the biggest stumbling block to bringing a new ministry into the church is the lack of leadership to carry it out. It becomes another to-do item on the pastor's already overloaded list. Avenue provides live training, comprehensive help, and ongoing resources to help you carry out this role without burdening your church or pastors.

If your church isn't ready to offer this ministry corporately, you may still be able to hold group meetings there. The church would not be responsible for getting word out about the group. That would be your job as facilitator.

Even if your church decides not to offer Avenue ministry, the counseling pastor is likely aware of women who would benefit from such a group. As you make that pastor fully aware of the nature of the group and supply him or her with brochures from the leader's kit, the church may send a few women your way.

Another option is to find a location other than your church where you can hold weekly meetings. Most AA meetings are held this way around the country. Churches, schools, and business centers, even medical facilities, open their doors without cost to accommodate recovery groups. You might also consider your or a friend's office building or someone's home if you know the attendees well.

BIG OR SMALL, IT WORKS

No matter which venue you choose, the group process is the same. With your group together, your guidebook will lead you in a safe environment where you will be understood and loved in the midst of your situation. Avenue's healthy group dynamics offer an opportunity to try on new ways of expressing your feelings, learning the art of confrontation, finding your own voice to express long-silent thoughts, and marking the end of isolation and shame. Consider a few more letters from women who just completed an Unintended Journey group course.

Natalie: I entered Avenue about three years after discovering my husband was addicted to porn. It really helped me to stop focusing on him and trying to control his recovery. It helped me to start discovering myself and what I needed. I had what I would call "raging codependency," not only with my husband but also with my children. Although I have not completely healed from this, I have made great strides in discovering my own feelings and establishing boundaries. I have hope that God will heal me. I don't know what the future holds for my relationship; yet I know I'm in a better place than I was five months ago.

Leslie: My husband and I raised our two children in the knowledge of the Word. In 1995 I was diagnosed with breast cancer. My husband was there for me, but somewhere in the process of my recovery, the Enemy worked his way into our lives through my husband. He was no longer interested in church and began to verbally attack me, and I began walking on eggshells in my home. He didn't want to be around family. He convinced our children I was losing my mind. My children were having a hard time seeing the truth. I began doubting myself, and he urged counseling in order to cover up an affair.

One evening I came home to find him in a dark house with my daughter's girlfriend. I had prayed one week earlier, *Lord, reveal the truth. If I am sick, help me. Whatever Dave is doing, bring it to light so no one could deny it.* God heard my prayer. The last nine months have been an inconceivable journey. The pain at times was more than I could bear. The details of this pain are slowly fading in my new awareness of God's truth and promises. Through Avenue, He has met my need, and my love for Him is greater than I've ever known.

Avenue provided a safe environment and a shelter. A small group of ladies related to my circumstances. It was exactly what I needed. Each circumstance was different, but we all experienced common red flags, denials, betrayals, and abuses. Women need a safe place to share without fear of judgment, and through Avenue I have reclaimed my body, soul, and spirit through God's truth. "Not that I speak from want, for I have learned to be content in whatever circumstances I am" (Philippians 4:11, NASB). To God be the glory.

Christine: I am still just beginning my journey and don't know where God will lead me. I discovered that my husband of twenty years is gay and has had numerous affairs. The pain is huge. He was very clever and left no clues about his dual life. I have since discovered that his first lover was in our wedding party. I thought he was a dear friend to be trusted. Two years ago his marriage tanked when his wife discovered his secret life. Only God knows what will happen to us. I doubt the marriage will survive. I will offer it up as a sacrifice to God—it was my dearest treasure. Thank you for publishing this excellent, excellent guidebook. I plan to toss my own loss stones into the sea this summer. Please pray for us and our three lovely children.

Jessica: My husband told me he had been with another woman and that I needed to get tested for STDs. He also admitted to watching porn for the past four years on our home computer. My reaction: I could care less if I had AIDS. I wanted to die. I felt betrayed; he had broken our wedding vows, and our marriage was ruined. I felt unloved. How could he do these things and still tell me he loved me? He is a liar. I felt like a fool. I believed I was his one and only, the one he cherished. I felt dirty. How could I have been so deceived? His actions greatly damaged my self-worth.

A few days later, we went to see our pastor. He asked my husband if he thought he was addicted to pornography. When he said yes, I was shocked. I had never heard of such an addiction. Our pastor directed my husband to Avenue for Men. I read a book about infidelity. We asked two couples in our church to come alongside us for accountability.

My husband was very repentant and accepted God's forgiveness. He had been living a double life; now he was growing in the Lord. But I was very confused. I wanted to help my husband, but I didn't know if I could, or even if I should trust him again. Prayer helped, but I needed to talk with other women who understood my hurt. When I heard of Avenue for Women, I called, and at the group I met some of the most precious ladies I have ever known. This program has saved my sanity, increased my faith and dependence in God, restored my self-image, and given me hope for the future. Many thanks to the group facilitators; they truly gave of themselves to us. And thank you, Sandy, for allowing God to work through you.

Sandy: I had a great gift given to me at a time of crisis in my life. That gift was Avenue for Women. When I started my journey, the Lord was very clearly not in my life. When I would see a car with a Christian fish, I would say, "There goes another Jesus freak." My heart had been hardened by years of not knowing what was wrong with my life. I was married to a man with a twenty-five-year sexual addiction. I had begun to think our life was "normal" because I no longer knew what was normal. When I discovered my husband's secret, I was completely destroyed. I fell to my knees and cried out, "If You are there, God, why did this happen? Why didn't I have any idea it was going on?" I then heard the voice that changed my life. He said, *I've always been here, Sandy, but you never listened.* I felt such calm and peace in that moment, and I was then able to move forward.

Through a series of God-placed connections, my husband and I found Avenue ministry. I was blessed and amazed that there were so many women just like me. What a treasure to be in a group of women to whom I could speak freely in a completely safe environment. I found my favorite word attending Avenue classes. That word is *hope.* Please know there is hope and healing through Christ and the help of Avenue ministries.

I cannot encourage you enough to get involved in Avenue. You will find comfort and healing through fellowship, Scripture, and an amazing development of your relationship with Christ. You will be in a safe and confidential group of women like yourself. You will be taken through boundaries, forgiveness, and other tools to help you walk this unintended journey.

I became a class facilitator and later administrator for Avenue for Women at our church. It was an honor and blessing to watch women come in broken and leave healed and able to continue their lives, confident of their strength. May the Lord be your hope through this journey and the hope for your healing.

Lest you think I solicited Sandy's endorsement, the only thing I requested of her was her own story, in her words. It is obvious that part of her story is her becoming a woman passionate about others finding the hope she once lived without. She's a smart, discriminating woman not easily persuaded by the latest trend. Her praises go to God, Rock of Ages, who appropriates Avenue to help people find Him.

Incidentally, Sandy became an awesome leader and a personal friend. I handed my *baby* over to her, the first Avenue chapter, which we birthed in our home church. I needed to move into a new role as director of women's ministries, overseeing all the Avenue women's groups. When I asked her and she accepted, she took on that role with some experience and with lots of passion and wisdom. She is the epitome of a great leader and has the heart of a servant. I have had the honor of learning from her how to better serve those God has called me to.

I pray that as you take the hand of help Avenue is extending, you find the support you need on this unintended journey, redeeming what was lost, rebuilding the ruins, discovering new treasures, and experiencing joy again.

17

A Little Bit About Facilitating a Group

When I birthed that first group, it wasn't because I was looking to lead a group. I was just trying to help other women find a supportive group like I had with my own friends. Over the previous year, my husband had formed the first men's group, and during that time, I was approached here and there by the wives of the men attending it. I didn't have much to offer other than hope and what I had been learning myself. I felt like I was just two steps ahead of where they were.

After a time, I realized they needed to come together; a sense of community was missing. I knew all these women, but they didn't know each other, and I couldn't manage any more one-on-one conversations. I had a toddler to chase after and a design business to manage. So I spoke to the women's ministry pastor at our church and suggested that *somebody* should start a women's group for all these wives. I figured she might do it since she held my hand while I went through the first weeks of grief over my husband's issues. The first words out of her mouth were, "Sounds like God is calling you."

I was dumbfounded. I had no skills, no experience, and no training to lead a group. But she encouraged me, gave me some sound advice, and sent me to "go forth."

So I did—in fear and trembling. There was no study guide, no leader's guide to follow. For "curriculum" I pulled together copies of things I had read that were helpful to me and scriptures that guided me. I wrote down a few things extracted from my journal, gathered a few questions to get conversation going, and prayed. For our first meeting, about fifteen women showed up. That was a crowd; I hadn't expected so many. I started our time together with prayer, and then we were rolling.

There was no lack of dialogue. Women were hungry to know other women who were in the same mess. I carried on in that fashion to facilitate the group for about five years, piecing together specific issues to discuss from my own reading and insights.

It was when other churches asked me to speak and wanted our help and our curriculum to start new groups that the next phase began. This time I was aware that God was talking to me. I made copies of all my pathetic handwritten notes and passed them out with apologies.

But God was giving us His bigger vision—to be a resource, a beacon of hope, an *avenue* to His healing, throughout this country. We set about getting organized as a ministry, and Clay and I spent a year writing the guidebooks and leader's guides. Those prior years of learning on our knees were poured into those books. Information that we had nowhere but in our heads was put to paper so we could swiftly, and without apology, hand this resource to anyone wanting to help or to be helped.

I offer this history to encourage you. If I initiated a group with nothing but some hope and a prayer, how much more equipped will you be with hope, prayer, and guidebooks?

You may doubt you're qualified, but if you're willing to consider the possibility, you will discover that having everything together is not important in facilitating a group. The primary requirement is being willing to give some of your time—but not much more than attending the group and working on the week's chapter.

People tend to get hung up on the word *leader*. We use the title *facilitator* for a few reasons. A facilitator is not expected to teach, advise, or counsel. Rather, she *facilitates* the creation, hosting, safety, and rhythm of the group meetings. The leader's guide lays out the guidelines for leading the group. It will get you started and help you troubleshoot any circumstances that arise. The other "leader" is the Bible, doing the job of teaching and advising. The facilitator's tasks are to adhere to the schedule, keep discussion on topic, and enforce basic group courtesies.

The group courtesies are listed in the leader's guide and reviewed during the first week of the group. The leader's guide offers tactful, gentle ways to *facilitate* the group process.

Coaching meetings via biweekly telephone conferences are also available as a service to our facilitators. Every two weeks, facilitators and other Avenue leadership call in to the meeting, and the coach discusses a specific topic to help you hone your facilitating skills, followed by Q and A. During the days between coaching calls, when a question comes up, you can e-mail it to the coach, and she will answer the questions in the following conference. To learn more about how to take advantage of the Teleconference Leadership Coaching (TLC), visit our Web site, AvenueResource.com

Here's what one woman had to say about facilitating her first Avenue group:

Mandy: I have learned that we have the awesome opportunity to witness the healing hand of Jesus. How wonderful He is to let us, who don't deserve this, view and even take part in the miracle of healing hearts. I am blown away that I could ever be a part of His plan. I picture the God of the universe swooping through our church, our group, and leaving us breathless when we see the wind of His work moving through! It astounds me.

Mandy's words reveal her heart. She's not relying on any talent she may have as an instructor to "fix" women; she's expressing what God will do when two or more are gathered together to seek Him. I interviewed several facilitators to offer more insight into this unique honor. Here are just a few of the responses.

At what point in your personal healing did you become a facilitator? Were you completely "fixed" before you were able to facilitate?

Beth: About a year and a half after I went through the group for my needs. I cofacilitated with a very experienced facilitator. Hmm, was I fixed? Well, most of my identity was still all about him. "Was *he* fixed? Was *he* acting out?" My hubby was in recovery, and things were quieting down. I was healed of my pain (pretty much), but all the issues that surround the family system take a long time to undo, I think. So, no, I wasn't fixed.

Carol: I started facilitating a group in order to have one to attend. I was trying to figure out my difficulties by reading various books. While visiting an out-of-town Christian bookstore for more resources, I overheard the store's owner telling another woman about the Avenue materials and the great things she had heard about the groups. So I asked her and found out there wasn't a group in my little town. But I felt this was something I really needed. I got the leader's guide and the guidebook, and then I told the women's ministry leader at my church that I would like to start the group. She was willing to put it in the Bible-study listings, and several women signed up. Also, I invited a neighbor who was divorcing because of her husband's affair.

Ann: I began facilitating within a year of first attending my support group. I just said yes. I had learned to trust God and the woman who invited me to facilitate. She had been one of my facilitators. She paired me with this wonderful woman, and we had such different stories. We prayed together and talked at least once a week to pray for the women and plan our sessions. It was a joy. I was far from fixed. I think I was facilitating in my second group when my husband relapsed. Facilitating seems to work best when engaged in one's own healing journey. We are facilitating God's work of healing, and it is all God's power. It just kept strengthening my walk with God and other women.

Joy: I facilitated a new group right after the one I attended was completed. I was absolutely not healed. One is never "fixed," as though there is some point at which you arrive at that place of perfection. No matter what life hands me, though, I've learned how to make decisions that are healthier and spiritually sound.

Debbie: Well, it was about six months after the group I participated in ended. I was still recovering from my husband's death, which happened while I was in that first group. I was still working on my own recovery, and I didn't feel I had much to offer. I felt I would be able to offer more if I had waited a few more months, but the Lord and my own facilitator said some things that changed my mind. I definitely was not fixed before becoming a facilitator. I knew how much Avenue had helped me, so I wanted to comfort others with the comfort God had given me through Avenue.

Beth, Carol, Ann, Joy, and Debbie offered additional perspective on the role of facilitating. If you would like to hear what else they had to say, visit the Avenue Web site, AvenueResource.com, and click on "Start Avenue at your church."

May God give you the seed of courage to put one foot in front of the other. May your heart and mind be always willing and listening for God's voice to give His direction and His timing to take each new step. May He provide you with good companions for the journey. May He protect you and yours as you make your passage into the unknown. May He infuse your soul with hope that can't be uprooted in tumultuous winds. May the acorn seed sprout into a mighty oak, whose name is righteousness. May your beauty display His splendor. May your restoration draw others to seek His healing touch. May He replace your mourning with joy.

About the Authors

BRENDA STOEKER is the cofounder of Living True Ministries, whose mission is to practically elucidate God's truth and to encourage and equip men and women to rise up and *be* Christian, rather than to *seem* Christian. A respected teacher, Brenda has taught and counseled hundreds of couples in how to connect in intimate relationships with each other. She is also an award-winning author, having cowritten the ECPA's Silver Medallion winner *Every Heart Restored* with her husband, Fred, to whom she's been married for more than twenty-five years. Brenda resides with her family in Des Moines, Iowa. For more information on Fred and Brenda Stoeker's ministry, visit FredStoeker.com or write: Living True Ministries, P.O. Box 94065, Des Moines, Iowa, 50394.

SUSAN ALLEN is the cofounder of Avenue, whose vision is to pave the way to help, hope, and healing from sexual brokenness. Though Susan is naturally inclined to the environmental design arts, God instilled in her a passion to write specifically for women who find themselves on a similar unwelcome path to the one she has taken. Her guidebook, *Unintended Journey,* has formed the heart of hundreds of women's peer-support groups across the country. For comprehensive information on the resources of Avenue, please visit AvenueResource.com. Together with Clay, her husband of twenty-five years, they enjoy life in Northern California with their family and friends.

A True Compass to Guide You Beyond the Devastation of Broken Trust

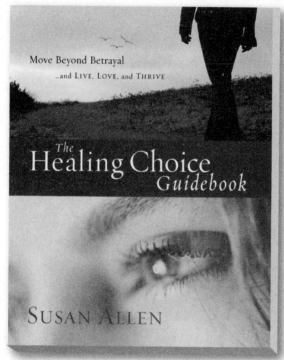

This powerful companion to *The Healing Choice* walks you through the process of personal healing, leading you to grow deeper in your relationship with God and equipping you to find healthy support in the company of other women who understand your pain.

Trade hope and healing for your brokenness

About Avenue Ministries

An interdonominational non-profit ministry founded by Clay and Susan Allen, AVENUE exists to offer healing to men caught in the snare of sexual compromise, and to wives devastated by betrayal.

To locate an AVENUE chapter in your area, or to begin one at your chuch, call 877.326.7000 or visit the website at www.AvenueResource.com

---

About Living True Ministries

Under Fred and Brenda Stoeker's leadership, LIVING TRUE MINISTRIES operates on:

Vision:
To become a pivotal voice of reason in the midst of cultural decay.

Mission:
To practically elucidate God's truth, encouraging and equipping men and women to rise up and be Christian, rather than to seem Christian.

Values:
Integrity, Congruency, Character, Urgency, and Normality.

If you are interested in a live appearance by Fred Stoeker, or for additional information, please email fred@fredstoeker.com or visit www.FredStoeker.com or www.BrendaStoeker.com.